Confessions of a desperate doctor and dentist

Dr Ray Lowry

All Copyright © 2013 Ray Lowry

In UK: All rights reserved. Apart from any permitted use under UK copyright law, no part of this publication may be reproduced or transmitted in any form or by any means, electronic or mechanical, including photocopy, recording, or any information, storage and retrieval system, without permission in writing from the publisher or under licence from the Copyright Licensing Agency Limited.

In US: All rights reserved. Except as permitted under the United States Copyright Act of 1976, no part of this publication may be reproduced or distributed in any form or by any means, or stored in a database or retrieval system, without the prior written permission of the publisher.

ISBN-13: 978-1482760057

ISBN-10: 1482760053

DEDICATION
This book is dedicated to
Loraine, Katy and Jess
who will be relieved to know that
they do not feature in these pages.

This book covers two distinct periods in my life: first as a dentist, second as a medic. The content reflects the two different worlds. The first (dental) half is heavy with descriptions of practical procedures, both learning them and carrying them out. This is the world of dentistry: very hands-on, small scale and detailed. The second (medical) half of the book is less technical and more anecdotal. That is what being a doctor involves, at least at the level covered in these pages. So if you are after stories don't get bogged down in the technical pages – move on and you'll soon find a tale or two. If you want to know more about the dental/medical trade, dwell on the technical pages between the yarns.

Disclaimer

This book is based, in part, on actual events, real people and former organisations but most characters and incidents used herein are fictitious. Any similarity between these characters, incidents or organisations and any actual person, living or dead, or to any actual event, or with any existing organisation is entirely coincidental and unintentional.

ACKNOWLEDGMENTS

Many thanks to Helen Bowman (In the detail www.in-the-detail.co.uk) for editorial support; and to Kevin Morley (kevart@hotmail.co.uk) for the cover artwork.

Thanks to all those who have contributed to these tales: the people who are in them (though you won't be able to identify yourself); family, friends and colleagues who have encouraged me; enemies and those who did me wrong for the opportunity to wreak revenge; and all those who have helped me develop the stories (audiences, fellow writers and performers).

1

Never trust an author that makes you read a quotation at the beginning of a chapter. He is up to no good.
A*o*

I always imagined I would start my memoirs something like this:

'Hugh G Rection leant back in his chair, drew on his pipe and sucked a large blob of foul-tasting goo into his mouth. This made life extremely difficult for him. First he was on the interview panel for prospective dental students at Newcastle-under-Brine dental school, confronted by eminent colleagues (several of whom envied his position as senior lecturer in oral surgery, most of whom were his sworn enemies) and a nervous sixth-former in the middle of his interview. So any attempt to deal with the goo in the normal way - a damn good spit accompanied by vigorous and noisy hawking in the throat - was out of the question. Under more congenial circumstances, he would have quipped that he found himself in the classic dilemma: to spit or swallow.

Second, the goo was so foul that it had to go one way or the other - out of his mouth, or down into his stomach. He'd had experience of the latter before and he did not relish the thought of it. The last time he'd swallowed the tarry mass he had indigestion so badly that he was forced to cut back on the whisky.

So there was only one way for it to go. But it had to be discrete. The problem was, the longer it dwelled in his mouth the more it burned its way into the lining of his cheek. So with as quick and casual a manoeuvre as he could engineer he despatched the mess into his handkerchief. But he felt so relieved to get rid of it that he let out an involuntary 'yesssssss'. That startled the Dean of Dentistry, who had just asked the panel if anyone had any further questions. So Hugh felt obliged to ask one. But even he was surprised by the falsetto sound that came out of his mouth. He learnt one more interesting fact about oral physiology that day - tobacco goo can turn you into a cartoon character'.

There are obvious flaws in the approach. Firstly, it is unmistakably a work of fiction. Think about it: how could I possibly know what was going on in the interview room let alone in the mind of an obviously-fake character like Hugh. And there is not, to my knowledge, a place called Newcastle-under-Brine. There is a Newcastle on Tyne and I spent a lot of my professional life there so why fictionalise it?

Besides it is now completely inconceivable that people would have smoked a pipe in an admissions interview for a British University dental school even back in the days when I went there. I did witness an anaesthetist putting people to sleep while smoking a cheap cigarette (he rested it on the gas machine between puffs). It was a miracle we weren't blown sky high. Modern day dental people will be embarrassed to be reminded of their wayward predecessors so that also makes the passage passé. Furthermore I don't know about you but I can't stand fictionalised memoirs.

Secondly, what really happened to me is much funnier than any dramatized version. What follows is an embellished account of what actually took place when I studied medicine and dentistry from the late 1960s to the mid-1980s. What I describe didn't just occur to me, but I reassure contemporary patients and colleagues that they have been disguised beyond recognition. I have taken liberties with the incidents, partly to conceal the place, time and players, and partly for entertainment purposes - I spend some of my life in retirement plying audiences with tales of those far off days so I have to spice it up a bit to keep them awake and earn my fee. But it's up to you to decide how much is fact and how much is fiction. There really was a Ray Lowry, I really did study dentistry at Birmingham and medicine at Leicester. And I really was desperate.

This book is called 'Confessions of a desperate doctor and dentist' because, like any young man of my age and in my era, I was desperate in the nicest possible way. I was not a desperate criminal or anything unsavoury. I was nice-desperate, productive-desperate, motivated-desperate. For all those years my life was one long string of desperation. I was desperate to get through my exams, desperate to become a professional, desperate to find out my niche in life, desperate to grow up, desperate for sex. All of these things played on my mind (at reunions I'm told it dominated most of our minds). And I dare say most people felt the same at that time of their lives. I was just lucky that it all played out against a dental and medical backdrop.

2

What was a dental student like me doing with his index finger up this girl's bottom? I could lie to you and say her wisdom teeth were a long way back and badly impacted. You might well think I was just a dirty dentist out to fill the wrong cavity. Or that I was an amateur proctologist trying to keep my hand in. But no, it was much more innocent than you think. I was doing the poor girl a favour and there was nothing naughty about it whatsoever.

I was a second-year dental student at Birmingham University. It still surprises many people that dentistry involves a university education. Most folks imagine that dentists go to technical college where they learn to mix dental cement beside bricklayers, extract teeth with carpenter's pliers and drill like road menders. But dentistry has always needed a university degree. The apprenticeship is longer than most ordinary courses; four and a half years, nearly as long as for doctors and vets. And like our other clinical colleagues the early years were a gentle introduction to professional life. Nowadays I understand it's much more draining.

First and second years at university were the preclinical ones before we started doing real dentistry on actual people. We studied anatomy (the structure of the human body especially the mouth and surrounding structures), physiology (how it all worked as a biological system), and biochemistry (how the chemicals involved played their parts). So we would learn the muscles of mastication (chewing) in anatomy, study how they worked (the nerve supply, how the muscles contracted, their part in the digestion process) and how the accompanying saliva and its biochemistry helped taste, digestion and the lubrication of speech. We learnt all that for the head and neck and some of the body as well.

We did other subjects, like comparative anatomy. My dental school was very hot on comparative anatomy: man compared to ape, dental student to sloth, medical student to laughing hyena and so on. So all around the school - behind doors, in windows, and especially in the museum - there were skeletons and stuffed bodies of every animal imaginable. Except a lion. And one notorious night we got our lion and I was there.

The local zoo rang the medical school up and said, 'Look, our old lion is on his last – well, in fact, he's not on his last legs. He's on the floor. He's semi-comatose now. If you kill him, you can have his body.' So that was why, late one night, twenty mates and I were in the body store in the basement of the medical school to see this lion finished off.

But how do you kill a lion without ruining the body? You can't bang it on the head because you'd crack the skull. You can't electrocute it because all the fur flies off – no-one wants a nude lion. And you can't strangle it because you break the little bones in the neck, very important in comparative anatomy.

Then some bright spark at the back of our spectator group put his hand up. There's always a bright spark, isn't there?

He said, 'I'm an anaesthetist and we've got this new sedative – a very powerful sedative – in the department. We've got buckets of the stuff. We can't give it away. Why don't I inject a paw full of this and Bob's your uncle?'

We now know that this substance is an extremely powerful sedative in humans - but not in the cat family. It's a stimulant in the cat family. So our anaesthetist colleague administered a potent stimulant to the big slumbering cat while we're all stood round calmly watching.

After a lull the lion opened one eye. We all went, 'Ahh…'

Then it opened his other eye and we all went, 'Ooh!'

Then the Lion got to his feet and we all went, 'Oh, s**t!'

Finally it let out an enormous roar. So we went for the door.

Every animation cartoonist knows that twenty into one doesn't go; twenty people trying to beat everyone else through the only door is going to cause chaos. We were all arms and legs like a Tom and Jerry cartoon. Fortunately the effort of the roar killed the lion so there was no need for the panic.

Eventually, when we recovered our composure, we laughed and joked about our predicament. My classmate Leo said to me, 'What was all that pushing and shoving for, Ray? You couldn't outrun the lion.'

I said, 'I didn't have to outrun the lion. I just had to outrun you.'

The preclinical years were also time to experience university life in its widest sense before we evolved from unruly teenagers into mini professionals. Dental students metamorphose like insects, starting as undergraduate caterpillars and emerging as dental butterflies. The caterpillar-like new undergraduate is lazy, scruffy and eats and drinks junk. Then gradually, almost imperceptively, a change starts: senior dental undergraduates dress more smartly, start shaving (both men and women); they begin to eat healthier food and drink less alcohol; they party less and study more. They leave their wild days behind and become studious, serious, focussed. So we had fun before we transmuted.

After single-sex boarding school the new freedoms that university life offered were a revelation to me. I went to a minor public school so we were destined to rule in a minor way, as members of the clergy, as army officers, accountants, lawyers, schoolmasters, doctors and dentists, businessmen. But whatever our station in life some things we had in common with all prospective members of the establishment. We wanted to have sex. So when a girl I fancied paid attention to me, I thought my undergraduate time had come.

I met this ground shaking girl in the student's union theatrical society, the Guild Theatre Group. Before I went clinical I had time to indulge in hobbies and one of them was theatre. I'd done a lot of it at school, both acting and stagecraft; management, lighting, sound, set design and so on. It was an all-consuming hobby at school, so I naturally fell into more of it when a dental undergraduate, especially in the early years when I had plenty of spare time and a longing to do interesting things.

At GTG it was very professional. All the acting was done by drama students, so what was left for the likes of me was backstage.

However, no matter how much I engaged in backstage life, I found the actors more glamorous, more attractive and more interesting. The drama students all seemed so gifted and charismatic - a new and exciting breed I had never experienced before especially at first hand. And that was doubly-so for the female actors, the girl drama students. And there was one in particular.

Her name was Cloaca. She had a Mediterranean complexion, long black hair, a generous figure, and a smile to melt the heart of any public schoolboy. She was about my height. She wasn't at all glamorous – she dressed in scruffy jeans, baggy pullovers, she wore no makeup or perfume, and her skin was a bit acned. But she was so sexy.

Unfortunately, the two sides of Guild Theatre Group never mixed. Actors were the dominant group. The backstage staff knew their place hiding away up in the gods above the scenery, in the lighting box at the back of the theatre, or in the workshop. Actors had the run of the non-technical areas (rehearsal rooms, stage area, auditorium), and the technical team (mostly boys with a few token girls) had the run of everywhere else. But our main territory was the workshop and office.

The workshop was next to our office, a shambolic room littered with debris, dirty tea mugs, grubby ash trays, and lined by a collection of dilapidated chairs and sofas. These worn-out props were never thrown out until they actually became dangerous, drawing blood with a protruding spring or splintering a resting buttock with fatigued and unruly wood. The assorted furniture lining the walls was like a row of rotten teeth. As a dental student I felt quite at home in the office. But the actors never came into our domain, so I admired Cloaca from afar. But things suddenly took a turn for the better.

One day, completely out of the blue, Cloaca approached me. I was alone in a corridor backstage. She suddenly appeared round the far corner and walked towards me. I smiled and she ignored me as she always did. I turned round to watch her walk away from me, safe in the knowledge that I could admire her retreating rump without being reproached by her.

All of a sudden she stopped. She turned. Then she smiled at me and walked back. I was transfixed. I looked behind me assuming she was smiling at someone else. But we were alone. When I looked round she was close to me and smiling into my face. She touched my arm and asked me back to her place. She smiled again, turned, and I followed her out into the night and, I assumed, to almost certain sexual heaven. I found my parked Morris Minor 1000, and, in a daze, drove her to her home. I expected I was soon going to be deflowered.

She lived in a terraced house in Selly Park, a suburb of Birmingham just down the road from the student union which itself was on the edge of the main university campus. She gave me directions all while making pleasant chat. I didn't take in a word she said such was my state of euphoria. She asked me to follow to her house, showed me into the front room and said she would be back in a jiffy. I nearly passed out with anticipation. But when she came back, instead of getting down to business she told me the real reason that she asked me back.

She had been badly constipated and the doctor had given her a suppository to clear the backlog. Only she didn't fancy using it on herself. And the only medic she knew was me so she wanted me to administer it. She hurried me to get on with it. Before I had a chance to say anything, she handed me the suppository, pulled down her clothes and bent over. She adopted what in veterinary circles is called the Lordosis position, one that some mammalian females display when they are in heat and are ready to mate.

Whatever this position she and I were in was called, it was the first time I'd been in a situation like that with anyone in a position like that. So I did what I was told and shoved the suppository where requested with my index finger with, I hoped, enthusiasm and panache.

Unfortunately, suppositories have nasty side effects and she had one, noisily and with a nasty smell. Cloaca quickly regained her composure. She sat up, pulled up her clothes and rushed out of the room with an urgent look on her face. For the next ten minutes I was embarrassed to hear straining noises from the downstairs toilet. Eventually she popped her head round the door, apologised for having taken up my time, thanked me for helping her 'get a result' and bundled me out the house before I had a chance to say anything coherent.

My virginity had to stay intact for a while longer. That made me more desperate than I had been before. Perhaps if I had had a more conventional introduction to the mysteries of the female plumbing I would have fared better. This episode reinforced many of the prejudices I had developed so far in my adolescence. Women were there to tempt innocents like me. They could twist us round their little fingers. They could get us to do the most absurd things which we would do gladly if there was a chance of sexual favours. And they could snatch them from our grasp at the last minute leaving us frustrated and bewildered.

Yet I knew as I sulked back to my car that I would come back for more, another time, another place when again I would do almost anything for my chance at sexual satisfaction. I really was a hopeless case of desperation.

Because of my experience with Cloaca I never developed a taste for anything remotely to do with suppositories or where they are destined to go, much to the relief of future girlfriends. But I was petrified of having sex with girls for some time afterwards. I long suffered from a bad case of flatus interruptus.

3

Like any other profession, there are rites of passage for dentistry: your first inferior dental local anaesthetic injection; the first time you take a tooth out; sawing a human head in half to examine the corpus callosum of the brain. But the primary rite is to get into a dental school and it looked as though I was about to fail miserably at that. I was on foot making my way to Birmingham Dental School and I was struggling.

My brown school-issue Duffel coat was no match for the Birmingham wind. My face, the only exposed part of me, was numb and paralysed as if I'd had a complicated stroke. This had only happened to me once before when I tried Saki, a very strong Japanese wine. Then I had been very drunk and inscrutable; now I was sober and miserable. I had a face as stiff as a wicket-keeper's glove but I couldn't give up.

I tried to make headway but my satchel, light with my meagre personal papers, strained angrily backwards downwind like an airport windsock in a hurricane trying to decapitate me. I was struggling to get to my one-and-only interview for dental school; it was the only offer from the many schools I had applied to. So I had to make it but it was turning out like a film starring the old time movie comedians Buster Keaton and Laurel and Hardy.

I'd always liked silent comedy but wasn't laughing now, and not just because of my paralysed face. I was late and the wind was playing havoc with my progress.

Just to stay still I had to lean forward like Buster Keaton in a tornado. One of the buildings I was passing was the office of the Birmingham Evening Mail newspaper and discarded pages from the loading bays kept blowing in my face just like Oliver Hardy trying to read a roadmap in an open top car. I was getting nowhere, jutting forward at an impossible angle my face covered in newsprint.

I was beginning to think that this was some sort of perverse aptitude test, to weed out all the weak prospective dental students even before they were interviewed. I was just about to give up when the wind suddenly stopped and I dropped to the floor like a stalled aeroplane precipitously deprived of lift. At least the newspaper debris broke my fall.

Now here's a fascinating thing. If I had looked at the television page of the Evening Mail on that day, and if I was clairvoyant, I would have seen that the programmes on that night would still be on forty years later. Such is progress that the television programmes from that era have survived long after the dental materials and techniques I was to study had been consigned to the dustbin of history.

I pressed on to the dental school but it was nowhere to be seen even though I was good at navigation. In my last years of school I had been in the Royal Air Force flying corps. Once a week we senior boys had played at being soldiers, sailors or aircrew. As a ploy to get us interested in joining the armed forces, it gave us a chance to sample the life in a watered-down form especially the toys. So we shot real guns, sailed real boats (on a pond, not the sea) and flew gliders.

I ended up with a flying scholarship where the RAF paid for me to have flying lessons, so I knew my way around a map. I could fly a plane in cloud, navigate around a mountain and land in a monsoon but I couldn't find a ten floor dental school in the centre of a midlands' city.

The dental school was three miles from New Street, the main railway station. But when the city planners had razed the area to build the dental school they used the left-over space to fabricate a concrete and Tarmac motorway with lots of walkways, underpasses and palisades. It was easy get around in a car – in fact that was the whole point. On foot, that was altogether different. When it eventually came into view you could definitely see what looked like a dental school. But you couldn't walk directly there.

As far as I could see you had to get to the front door of the dental school by stealth, a sort of complex set of manoeuvres usually found in championship chess. If you took the direct route you would be dead, mown down by speeding cars on the urban motorway. No, as I found now by trial and error, you had to take a walkway one hundred yards to your right, then an underpass back a quarter of a mile. Next you would sprint across a motorway and climb over a wall. Down a flight of stairs you would have to go next past defaced murals, obscene graffiti and mountains of assorted litter.

I worked out how to do this and finally I emerged from a tunnel and there I was. Like Sir Edmund Hillary and his conquest of Mount Everest I had reached the first base camp, the ground-level doors. Perhaps I was going to pass the aptitude test after all.

There has been a dental hospital in Birmingham since 1858 but the one I was looking at now had been opened in 1963, four years before I arrived. The ten story building was state-of-the-art in its day but materials used in its construction (like asbestos) would soon become obsolete and its cozy nooks and crannies would eventually cramp the style of modern dentistry. But in its day, and certainly when I saw it for the first time that day, it looked impressive. The building was plastered with attractive tiles. I didn't know it at the time but in the years to come those tiles would begin to fall off, at random, making it a pedestrian hazard and the object of many a claim on staff car insurance policies. To me it looked awe-inspiring so I was keen to get inside

There were a number of entrances to the dental school. One door was designated Patients. A group of people huddled around the entrance looking nervous and furtive, I assumed plucking up the courage to go inside to face their denture maker. Many were having a last drag on their cigarettes.

The patients were all shapes and sizes. Those going in looked nervous, anxious, even frightened; those coming out looked relieved and many spitting blood. There were the obviously poor; the impoverished middle classes; the elderly with ill-fitting dentures; people with swollen faces, crooked noses complementing teeth fractured in fights or accidents. There were solitary people with noxious gum disease and halitosis. There were people with unsightly teeth, with no teeth, a few teeth, and too many teeth.

Some people had swollen faces or lumps in their necks. There were lips and palates that were cleft, noses that were crooked, chins that were regressive, faces that were asymmetrical. There were people with general medical complaints: with limps, paralysed limbs, blue lips, yellow eyes, flushed cheeks. And there were people who looked completely out of place because they had nothing obviously wrong with them, dental or otherwise. This last group rummaged through their appointment cards anxiously, obviously checking they were in the right place, before joining everyone else in the jostle to go in the door.

Those going in and out of the Staff entrance were equally unusual but in a different way. There were old men with severe stoops and thick glasses. I later learnt they were clinical dental tutors dilapidated by long hours checking on drilled cavities in the dim mouths of student patients.

The next group at this entrance were more distinguished men, well-dressed in frock coats with buttonholes in their lapels. They would turn out to be the consultant dentists, staff at the top of the tree in the clinical world. The final group I assumed were academics by their absent-minded demeanour and their mortar boards and gowns.

The entrance marked Nursing Staff was of particular interest to me coming from an all-boys boarding school. Most girls going in were young and attractive, lively, giggling in groups, a few bashful but most confident and vivacious. Some were more stern and forbidding; obviously the officer class of nurse, the sisters and matrons.

Finally I found the Student entrance. There were a few of the young people loitering there who looked older, more restrained, who had shorter hair, were clean shaven, more smartly dressed and carried briefcases. I guessed these were senior students. But the majority of the throng were young like me.

I stuck out like a sore thumb. I was pasty from months of A level examination revising indoors, spotty from puberty and I wore a suit that was obviously brand new for the occasion.

I sneaked in through the door and tried to find my way to the interview without attracting too much attention. I found myself in the basement of the dental school. Ahead of me were two sets of swing doors, one marked male and the other female. The changing rooms. Dentists started to wear the costumes of their profession after a couple of years so distinguishing them from run-of-the-mill students. The social pressure to conform began early.

There was not much else in the basement - a few noticeboards, a set of stairs leading up, and doors leading to the maintenance areas, anonymous doors with humming machinery inside or the hissing of escaping gas. I wondered if it was laughing gas and whether I would soon be paralysed by chemically-induced mirth. Knowing my luck, it would be coal gas and I would be choking not laughing.

There was one other feature of the basement that was completely new to me. The notice by it called it a Paternoster. It was a continuous lift, a series of compartments or open-fronted mini lifts. As far as I could see you jumped on and off the apparatus to go up or down. At the appropriate floor I guessed you would make a judgement and time your move on and off to coincide with the continuous upward or downward motion of the series of booths, each big enough to hold two people.

Years later, this sort of hazardous contraption would be severely curtailed on health and safety grounds, but, at that time, it looked a lot of fun. Not only was it like riding a funfair attraction, but, to an astute voyeur like me, I could see the great potential to look up the skirts of ascending girls, safe in the knowledge that their heads disappeared upwards before their hemlines.

There were signs directing me up to my interview. As I climbed the stairs I dawdled on each floor to take in the layout of the building noting the signs and wondering what each new name meant. The first floor was administration: there were signs for dental school directors, the senior common room, secretaries to the Dean, head of services and so on. Floor two was a clinical floor: oral surgery, extractions, oral medicine and related techniques. The third floor was more surgery but this time with an operating theatre, general anaesthetics area and 'recovery bays'. I continued on up. The fourth and fifth floors were signposted as conservation, periodontology and oral medicine. The sixth floor was more periodontology. The seventh, the last, housed laboratories, pathology and materials.

As I got higher I got more light-headed. The staircase was right next to a complete wall of glass that stretched from the ground to the tenth floor. The steps were open with gaps at the back. The bannisters were thin metal struts supporting a narrow metal and plastic handrail. It was all very flimsy-looking. It had been contemporary in its time, minimalistic, but it made me giddy as if I were starring in the Alfred Hitchcock film 'Vertigo'. And I didn't know where to go to get away from the dizziness – all these departments and offices were new to me so I daren't stray to find sanctuary.

I just had to keep pushing on up the stairs trying not to look down. It didn't help that I had on my new pair of leather-soled shoes and they were slippery as hell. I had to hang on to the rail very tightly. When I reached the top I must have looked like a climber reaching the summit of Mount Everest who was suffering extreme oxygen deprivation. I was speechless with the effort and the thin air. It took me a while to recover but the ascent had its compensations.

From this vantage point, seven floors up, I could see Birmingham laid out below. It was giddy-making being so high up and seeing so much of the city in miniature outside the big picture windows. You could appreciate the anatomy of the city from up here.

Birmingham was obviously an industrial city but in a hotchpotch layout. Unlike cities that had grown up round a cathedral it had developed piecemeal as many small businesses flourished. There was a jumble of buildings housing a mishmash of industry. Small metal-bashing family firms rubbed dirty shoulders with larger engineering conglomerates while one-man jewellers sat cheek by jowl with car repair shops and chemical works. The chaos wasn't even organised.

I suddenly realised that I had let my curiosity get the better of me. My interview was not up there. I retraced my steps down stairs still wary of the Paternoster. I managed to walk down without looking where I was going and it was lucky I wasn't spotted by anyone on the admissions panel as I looked as though I was partially sighted and afflicted with a stiff neck.

Eventually I found the notice I was looking for – 'interviews for prospective dental students'. I had missed it on floor one. It signposted the administrative wing of the building. The arrow pointed along a quiet corridor to what turned out to be the Dean's office.

I reported to the sullen secretary – she had obviously seen more prospective dental students than she cared for. She checked my name off the list and I sat by myself on a row of chairs in the empty corridor. Just opposite was a door marked 'Boardroom'. I guessed that was where I was going next. All around, in muffled silence, people worked away in offices. There were no signs of dentistry, not even a smell to show it happened nearby. I waited to go in to my interview.

Sitting outside in the corridor area was the first time I'd thought seriously about what they would ask in the interview. I presumed they would query why I wanted to be a dentist. Now I couldn't be sure. It was more like I didn't want to be a doctor or a vet. I vaguely wanted a medical career without the difficulties (the on-call, death and serious illness, bad smells, sick people). I wanted glamour, money, job satisfaction. I assumed being a dentist would give you all that without the pressures of a medic. So I rehearsed a few generalities that I thought would pass as reasons: I wanted to do good, I had a fascination for the mouth, I was good with my hands. I am sure they had heard them all before but I thought they would do.

The next question I thought they would ask was 'why Birmingham'. At first I supposed it would be easier to be honest: that it was my birth city, I liked the place, I loved the accent and this was all I knew and so on. But then I thought those reasons would seem feeble. They were. I thought harder and suddenly understood that I knew no good reasons to choose Birmingham Dental School. I hadn't done my homework. I didn't know what distinguished one dental school from another.

Rattled, I rehearsed a few plausible banalities: that Birmingham had a good reputation as a dental school, the word on the street was it was a good university to study at, that Birmingham dentists were some of the best. I sweated even more when I realised they would see through this load of flannel in an instant.

I tried to reassure myself I was in with a chance. I was well turned out, smart, clean and tidy. I had a few banalities ready and I could say them with a smile. All I needed was to empty my bladder for the last time just before I was called in to the interview room.

I found a toilet nearby. After I had relieved myself I felt a bit self-conscious. Like all men I was lazy. I didn't see the point of washing my hands after every act of micturition. That would have been overdoing it, even a bit effeminate, at least in my world of late-teenage boys living away from home.

Now I wasn't so convinced. Here I was about to be interviewed for a place in dental school. I had to persuade them I was good enough to be a dentist, and, I reckoned, dentists must have to have clean hands or at least go through the motions of keeping them clean. And I guessed that meant washing your hands after having a pee. And I wasn't completely sure they didn't have hidden cameras here in the dental school toilets to catch out dirty scruffs like me. So I thought I had better knuckle under and wash them this time, just for appearance sake.

Now I wasn't to know that most males in the dental school, whether dentist or not, didn't bother to wash their hands unless under the direct gaze of other people who might be prudish about the issue. So the tap in this toilet had not been used much, if at all, for many months. Which meant it was stuck. So I had to struggle with it to turn it on. That was my mistake.

When I gave it an extra twist to unjam it, it came unstuck all of a sudden and violently. This sent a hot stream of water shooting into the basin, and straight out again all down the front of my trousers. They were my best interview trousers, the ones I needed right now for my interview and they were soaking. And before I could do anything about it, I heard a loud voice outside the toilet calling my name and hurrying me to the interview room immediately.

The dental school had been built in the 1960s and the door to the boardroom was thick, dark wood with a contemporary handle and it was very heavy. Pushing hard, I opened the door as little as I dare, squeezed through, closed the door behind me and turned to look the boardroom. I don't know what to expect. I'd never been a real boardroom so my expectations were framed by popular culture. I had anticipated a room lined with panelling like the boardrooms in plays on television. But when I saw the real thing it was surprisingly modern.

The walls were lined with photographs and oil paintings of stern looking men. Some were in old-fashioned frock coats, most in lounge suits. One or two were in clinical white coats with dental instruments in their hands. They all looked dour, forbidding, stern, disapproving.

At one end of the room was a bookcase sparsely filled with silver cups and (presumably) dental artefacts: spears and shrunken heads from Africa, animal teeth, a tusk or two, and at least one frightening looking surgical instrument made of wheels, pulleys and handles decorated with ivory and mother-of-pearl.

In the middle and dominating room was a large heavy-looking wooden table big enough for professionals to play snooker on. Around the table sat the interviewers. There were six men and one woman. None of them smiled. They looked like a hanging jury at the assizes and I felt I was about to swing.

I tried my best to mask the large, steaming damp patch on the front of my trousers using my satchel, but it was too small, and I could see the interview panel had spotted something was wrong as I slid into the room. I sat with the satchel on my lap and resolved to keep it there all through the interview even though it was uncomfortable. I thought it would get me by without giving the game away. But the room was sweltering. I was nervous and became hot and sweaty. Almost straight away, steam started to rise from my lap. Soon my glasses were steamed up and I couldn't keep them clear even though I took them off and wiped them.

How I ever passed the interview I will never know, sitting there with a large, damp stain on my trousers as I stammered my inadequate answers through glasses rendered opaque by the rising steam. They admitted me, I was told later, because I had the nerve to stick it out, not to be put off by the discomfort or embarrassment. They also thought I needed a career that would give me practice turning on taps. Dentistry was the obvious choice.

4

Undergraduates have to live somewhere. At Birmingham University many first years could live in university-owned halls of residence. That campus was half a mile from the main University one in a leafy residential suburb of the city. It was a modern development, mainly low-rise bedsits and rooms with one high-rise block of flats set round the lake. It was like an Olympic residential village where competitors would be temporarily housed during the Games if staged in Birmingham.

Housing undergraduates together was a curate's egg, good in parts. The positive side was that the authorities knew where all the students were especially after they were in bed, for example on Sunday morning. But the downside of hot-housing so many young and volatile people was obvious. All those teenagers bottled up together meant that there were countless parties, much raucous behaviour, drinking and sex. There were also what were called hijinks: letting off fire extinguishers, throwing lifebelts into the lake, scrawling graffiti on walls and overturning of litter bins. But at least all the misbehaviour could be kept out of sight of ordinary Birmingham residents which pleased both the university authorities and the local city council.

Living in halls of residence was mainly confined to first year students. Some second and third years stayed in halls but as they grew older they could not all be accommodated there. Even more likely was that they would rather move out into flats, digs or squats with newfound friends. For medical and dental students, who had longer undergraduate courses than most, this meant that the vast majority lived outside halls of residence. I chose not to live in halls of residence from the very beginning.

I plumped for digs because I'd spent many years living at boarding school. When you've lived with many other people in crowded and cramped conditions you don't want to live with herds of other people any more. You begin to value your privacy. At first living in school was great fun and a big contrast to my early upbringing. It meant that we became sociable animals able to live in groups and survive, even be successful under some trying circumstances. For example multiple-occupancy slumbering was a challenge.

Sleeping with a lot of people sounded interesting in theory but wasn't in reality. The dormitory in a boy's boarding school, 20 to a room, is hardly the place for restful sleep. Of course the banter, pillow fights and practical jokes were great as a novelty but that soon wore off. It was only in the senior years when the numbers got smaller and your companions slept more soundly did you get the sleep you deserved. We didn't complain but it took its toll.

The other challenge to living at a boarding school was eating. We dined in the Grand Hall which accommodated the whole school, some 900 or so boys all eating noisily at the same time. It was the first time in my life that I'd ever eaten in a cacophony. To carry on a conversation with fellow diners at your table you needed to raise your voice above the others. The volume of noise in the hall gradually escalated during the course of a meal as all the boys tried to be heard above the rest. Table manners were also rather primitive as the food was dished out in a slapdash way. If you weren't assertive enough you could easily starve or be left with those bits of food that nobody else wanted.

So to have peaceful nights and to eat meals in peace and quiet I chose not to go into halls of residence. I looked for digs, a British arrangement where you would live in a house with a family often in a shared room usually on a bed and breakfast basis. After a little research guided by the university authorities I booked into a small residential home in the Selly Oak suburb of Birmingham. I first caught sight of my new living quarters when I turned up a day or two before the start of my first term at Mrs Bostock's house.

The house was a little semi-detached 1950s style dwelling in a quiet suburb about five miles from the University campus. I had struggled there on the bus after I had arrived in Birmingham on the train. I wasn't sure what to expect in a landlady so was pleasantly surprised when Mrs Bostock opened the door and I found she was a woman some years younger than my own mother and really rather attractive in a homely sort of way. She was warm and friendly and invited me in and, after taking various particulars and telling me the rules of the house, she shepherded me up a small flight of wooden stairs to what would be my room. The room had two single beds and she revealed that I would be sharing with another first-year dental student who had yet to arrive.

Leo Michaelson was my dig-mate and he was quite a different person from me. He had not been to boarding school and he had led a very sheltered life at home so moving into digs was a big step for him. He was naive and shy and I quickly found myself having to look after him and showing him the ropes which were very new to me as well. I wasn't much more experienced than him but in those days having a little bit more experience counted for a lot.

He was tall and thin, what's now known as gangly. He had bright red hair and a pale complexion blighted with acne, but even under all that he was not a handsome lad. I took some comfort that he might not compete with me for any potential sexual conquests – I'm afraid I saw life in these simple, crude terms in those days.

Leo was unworldly in many ways. He was an avid enthusiast for canals, the obsolete industrial transport system that featured in back-street Birmingham. He was also an enthusiastic collector and would bring canal memorabilia back to the digs after a weekend hobbying on the waterways. He caused a stir with one artefact he acquired when it turned out to be a vital water conservation device. Its absence was exposed through terrible flooding. I was sworn to secrecy while he buried the offending evidence in the Mrs Bostock's garden late one night.

Life in the digs was meagre but comfortable. In the days before our first attendance at the University we got used to the domestic routine. We would be mustered to breakfast at eight o'clock in the morning for cereal or toast and a boiled egg. At weekends we would be offered a more substantial start to the day such as scrambled egg on toast or bacon, egg and sausage.

Those first few days we spent our time exploring the local area: the shops, the transport, the cinema, the cafes, and, in the evening and very daringly, the local pubs. Even though I made out to be very different, in reality both Leo and I were inexperienced at going to the pub. Although I tried to be worldly and knowledgeable we were both obviously very amateurish when we ordered our drinks.

Me: 'What will you have Leo?'

Leo:' What is there?'

'Mild or bitter beer'.

'I'll have a medium'.

We sometimes had a snack in the pub, either crisps or scratchings (crisply-fried pork rind). We were equally indecisive about that.

'Leo, scratchings?'

'No, Ray, I've been using calamine lotion.'

'You'll be nuts then?'

'Watch it Mr Lowry'.

We were quickly intoxicated after a few glasses of beer and were worried that our landlady might be offended or, even worse, consider throwing us out when we returned to our digs.

Leo and I spent some evenings in together when we first started living at Mrs Bostock's. When you share a room with someone you end up doing the most childish things to pass the time before you go to sleep. One night Leo came in after a bath and his towel fell open. I was flabbergasted. He had one of the biggest penises I had ever seen and I had seen a few in my time at boarding school. He was quite casual about it but I was fascinated.

'You must be popular with the girls' is all I could say to get him talking about it.

'Not had much experience' was his reply. 'But I can't wait. Do you think it will put them off?'

'No, you'll be a popular lad and the envy of your male friends. How big is it, you know, when it is ready for action?'

'Never measured it and before you say anything we are not getting the rulers out here. I am not going to let you manhandle the thing no matter how curious you are.'

'Ok, but give me an idea. How many birds could roost on it when it is fully inflated?'

'Twelve'.

I was shocked and a little intimidated. 'Same here of course, I could get twelve birds on mine on a good night'.

'Yes, 'he said rather too knowingly I thought, 'but the end three would be flapping their wings'. I had to agree.

Years later Leo's organ became notorious. But just before we stopped sharing a room he invited a new girl back to our room and I had to pretend I was asleep while she seduced him. She had heard of Leo from a friend who had recommended him not for being well endowed but because he had strong religious beliefs. Her pillow talk gave the game away.

'Oh Leo, I'm so glad to have got you in bed. Now, get on top of me. I know you want my body and I hope you are not just going to talk about our mutual interest in BLOODY HELL.' Unfortunately Leo passed out soon after as too much of his blood went to inflate his manhood. She spend all night noisily trying to revive him, mind and body. I moved out soon after.

Like in the notorious seaside boarding house we were expected to stay out all day. This was easy in term time when we would be busy with our studies. During the day we had practicals and lectures. In the evenings we revised for exams. Most students in digs found somewhere to study after their lectures before they were allowed to go 'home' – the library was popular and even the students union had a few desks where revision could be done. I plumped for the medical school pathology museum. Each bay had a large table with six chairs. The walls were made up of shelves on which stood the jars containing the specimens. It was a distracting sight but was a welcome diversion from the boring work of revision.

During the day it was a golden rule we wouldn't go back to the digs but I did once break it absentmindedly. I came home to the digs in the middle of the afternoon. We respected that Mrs Bostock needed time to clean and service our room, shop, cook and look after her young baby. Her husband worked away so most weeks we had her to ourselves. She also needed time on her own. With us lodgers and her baby she had a full and busy household. So it was a welcome relief to her not to have us outsiders there during the day. But this day I assumed she wouldn't mind if I slipped in quietly and wasn't a nuisance. I was at a loose end and couldn't think what else to do.

I let myself in through the front door, closed it and hung up my coat. I was about to climb the stairs to my room when I heard a noise in the kitchen. It was muffled, but it sounded like Mrs Bostock talking to her baby. The baby appeared fractious and her voice was both soothing and anxious. She sounded frustrated. On the spur of the moment I thought she might like some company.

Except for meals I didn't normally go into the kitchen unless asked. Some parts of the house were partially out-of-bounds. The dining room, the kitchen, the lounge were all by arrangement only. Access to our bedroom was less restricted, as was the toilet and bathroom and the hallway. Mrs Bostock's personal rooms were way off limits. I popped my head round the kitchen door on my way up stairs.

There she was sitting at the kitchen table holding her baby in her arms. The kitchen was small and cosy warm. The Formica-topped table filled most of the space and today there was a large metal bowl on it with freshly-peeled potatoes soaking in water. There were four wooden chairs round it tucked in under it. When people were sitting in the chairs there was very little room to get around to serve food or to pass into the pantry.

There was also a gas cooker, a sink and draining board, a fridge and a sideboard with a let-down top that was fronted with opaque glass. A humble light hung from the ceiling with a fly paper dangling down from it. On a shelf on one wall was an old-fashioned valve radio. There was a picture on the wall of an oldish couple presumably Mrs Bostock's parents or grandparents, it was difficult to tell.

Mrs Bostock looked tired and flushed. She said she had tried everything to get the baby settled. 'Ray, I've tried rocking Dean, taking him out for a walk, singing to him. There's only one thing left. He can't be hungry, but I'll try anything.' I'd never seen her like this before. She was normally bright, efficient, organised and briskly maternal. Usually she was able to juggle us boarders, the baby, everyday living and whatever needed to be done in the house without batting an eyelid. But now she looked defeated. Both she and the baby had had about enough of each other.

Before I could say anything more she took out her right breast and began feeding little Dean. He settled straight away. I daren't move in case I disturbed them so I sat down trying to hide my embarrassment. I'd never been this involved with mother's milk since I was a baby myself. It was fascinating and disturbing at the same time. All I could do was stare.

Staring is a guilty pleasure. Most of us like to do it if we are allowed to which is rarely. As a society we frown upon staring, though it's in our nature to do it. At road traffic accidents we are urged not to slow down and stare. If there is a commotion in the street we are moved on by the authorities against our natural instincts to stand and stare. We crave it so much and are frustrated by not doing it that we have to seek it out especially; we pay a fortune to be allowed to stare officially at striptease clubs, in the theatre or the cinema. Satisfying our urges to stare is big business. But here I was getting it for free and was enjoying the novelty. What was going on before me was stare-worthy and I had a front row seat.

As the baby fed it relaxed and so did Mrs Bostock. Suckling seemed to settle him and as he got into a rhythm Mrs Bostock visibly unwound. She closed her eyes and a slight smile creased her face. Her neck went red and blotchy but she looked so peaceful. I felt very relaxed myself, what with the warm glow coming from mother and baby, the lovely smell, the soothing sounds and the contentment on display. It was a lovely sight to stare at.

Then Mrs Bostock started sniffling. I thought this was probably normal for breastfeeding but soon tears trickled down her face and I began to worry. What could be wrong? Was it me? She carried on feeding but, in between her cooing to the baby, she started to talk to me in a gentle, cracked voice. She was a bit hoarse, I assumed because she was getting a cold what with her sniffling. She said she was a little tired, hadn't been sleeping well and was missing her husband. She apologised for being emotional but she asked me to understand. I did. I didn't want her to stop what she was doing because I was enjoying it very much. This was what staring was intended for.

I suddenly realised I was enjoying it so much because I was staring at her naked breast. An alarm bell rang in the back of my mind. It was faint but persistent. It warned me that my staring was precipitously exposed. What had been immensely pleasurable, staring at her breast, was suddenly shameful. I didn't quite understand why as nothing seemed to have changed. I looked up at Mrs Bostock's face for an answer and saw she was staring back at me. But she didn't look annoyed or angry or upset. She almost looked inquisitive as if trying to figure out what was happening. And then she smiled.

'Have you never seen someone breast feeding before, Ray?' she asked. Her voice was soft and hoarse still, but in a different way. Her hoarseness now was deeper, coarser, more urgent and more visceral.

'No, I don't think so' I gulped, before I realised how pathetic that sounded. How could you be unsure about a thing like that, as if seeing someone breast feed was an everyday occurrence like reading a newspaper or buying a quarter pound of sweets? Her talking to me and staring back at me had caught me completely off-guard. I couldn't think straight let alone carry on a sensible conversation with her. I just made it up as we went along.

Then I don't know what came over me but I suddenly blurted out, for want of something to say, 'I've often wondered what breast milk tastes like, Mrs Bostock' as if talking about some obscure truffle or a rare wine. The question hung in the air as I squirmed with embarrassment at the crassness of the words.

'Why don't you find out Ray?' she said. I was immediately relieved thinking she meant I could look it up in a book or ask around at the University. Of course, how stupid of me, what breast milk tastes like is just the sort of thing we will cover soon in physiology or biochemistry. It's only a matter of time….. But the look on her face told me I was barking up the wrong tree.

I sat mesmerised during what came next. She disengaged the baby and put him down in his cot. He slept soundly. She came round the table and sat down next to me. She lifted up her bra and freed both breasts. She looked deep into my eyes and offered me the breast saying, 'Why don't you find out now?'

When you first do something complicated it helps to know what to do. We forget but walking, talking, eating and drinking were once very hard to do. We have to learn how to do those things; we didn't do them naturally, without lots of learning and sometimes instruction. Paradoxically, some things that are complex are innate like breast feeding especially in the young when they are vital to survival. But to an adult, if called upon do so at the drop of a blouse, it is long forgotten and not easy to do from first principles. That's why I found Mrs Bostock's kind invitation to try human baby milk on draught so perplexing. I didn't know what to do.

But I did my best. Not one to duck a challenge, I leant forward and took her nipple into my mouth. It was strange. Her flesh almost smothered me as I settled onto the nipple. I didn't realise that even latching on needed high levels of skill. How clever babies were to suckle and breath at the same time I thought. Then I sucked.

At first I sucked too hard. I drew both breast and nipple into my mouth like sucking in an enormous warm marshmallow. The nipple was firm so it felt like manoeuvring the valve of a deflated bicycle tyre. I pushed it out a bit with my tongue until I had the nipple only and then tried to suck. But I couldn't get any purchase. I tried to hold it firm between my teeth but Mrs Bostock flinched so I abandoned that idea almost immediately. I became flustered. I reckoned it wouldn't work if I sucked and it was no use blowing either. I was beginning to recognise a familiar feeling and it wasn't sexual. It was desperation, that old companion of mine. But what was I desperate for? I wasn't sure if I was desperate for it all to go on or to stop.

My indecision made me relax and some primitive suckling reflex kicked in. My mouth was suddenly filled with warm sweet milk. I had mixed feelings. Yes, I was enjoying it. But I was also worried that Mrs Bostock might have only wanted me to take a sip, like a professional wine taster. Perhaps I was to supposed to spit it out after my first breast full. I decided to carry on for a decent interval then gently disengage. But I was stumped for what was a decent interval to suckle milk when you were not the intended baby. What was polite? What was the etiquette?

Then I noticed Mrs Bostock was purring like a cat. She sighed and pressed my head more closely to her breast. I could hardly breathe. I couldn't completely surrender myself to the experience. Yes, it was surprisingly stimulating: the sensations, the smell, the emotion, the passion. But it was also disturbing, what with baby Dean lying asleep in his cot, me latched on to my landlady's exposed bosom and it was nearly tea time.

It was also very messy. Mrs Bostock was nuzzling me into her naked breasts which were responding by squirting copious amounts of milk all over my ears, hair, face and dribbling down onto my shirt. I was hot, bothered, aroused, confused and soaking wet.

Then we heard a key in the front door lock. I jumped back thinking the worse – that Mrs Bostock's husband had returned from his trip and that he would soon beat me to a pulp for violating his marital and fatherly rights. Mrs Bostock rapidly tried tucking her breasts back into her clothes and called out 'Who is it'. There was no reply but after a short interval the door to the kitchen slowly opened.

My fear turned to annoyance as I saw it was my roommate Leo. He had a bewildered look on his face partly because he had been caught breaking a house rule but also because I was in the kitchen in such a dishevelled state and Mrs Bostock had one breast in and other hanging out. He slowly recovered his composure and smarmed with a wide knowing grin on his face. All he could say was: 'That proves you're her favourite. Sucking up to her again are you Ray?' But he didn't notice the milky lino beneath his feet and he suddenly shimmied across the room knocking the bowl of peeled potatoes flying.

We all ended up looking foolish. My shirt front was soaking and I had milk-soaked hair. Mrs Bostock had her bra all tangled up and her breasts were squirting milk like an oil gusher. The baby tried to cry but a raw potato jammed in his mouth so he alternated a gasp and a retch. And Leo lay sprawled out on the floor with the upturned bowl on his head like a first world war infantryman.

We never mentioned the incident ever again. I also avoided milk at Mrs Bostock's digs for the remainder of my stay. You couldn't be too careful.

5

Birmingham was a very different place in the late 1960s when I started at dental school. But I didn't know any of that then. I had been born and brought up there until I went away to boarding school after the 11 plus, a long forgotten examination that used to split the nation's youth. If you passed it you went on to better schools in the state system. If you failed you were consigned to the educational scrapheap, treading academic water until you found low status employment when it was legal to leave school. If your parents could afford the private system, the 11 plus was irrelevant – you would be admitted to any school you chose as long as you had the cash.

I headed off to a private school where I boarded. I didn't have cruel or unusual parents who wanted to shunt me off their hands when I became an adolescent. It was more that the sons (and to an extent the daughters) of the professional classes were thought to be better groomed away from the temptations of ordinary working class children. So like many of my contemporaries I was shipped off to the public school situated in the depths of the countryside many miles from my home. There I stayed cocooned in a closed environment where I worked and played hard through a mixture of boredom and opportunity. So when I finally surfaced I had the academic qualifications to go to dental school but none of the worldliness to live in a metropolitan university city.

What a shock it was to find myself let loose in the city of my birth. I had never known it properly as a child. My sister and I were never allowed to roam freely or unaccompanied in any but a few choice locations mainly in the suburbs. The streets were safe to play in but we never went out of sight of our house. We did venture into town but these journeys were planned, heavily supervised and completely controlled. Those encounters had made me wary. A big city like Birmingham was a potentially hostile environment for a small boy like me.

Apart from its large scale there were the smells. Granted, there were a lot less fumes from cars and lorries than there are now. But there were pea-souper smogs that blanketed the city in winter when the air was almost clotted with smoke particles and soot from all the factory and domestic chimneys. At the city railway stations of Snow Hill and New Street the steam trains subjugated small schoolboys like me with their size, their noise but especially their smell; coal smoke and steam. Horses still worked in the streets with their accompanying aroma pulling delivery carts. Even at the docks in Liverpool where we used to catch the ferry to Northern Ireland on holiday, the air was stodgy with horse urine fumes;

horses were still used to do a lot of the heavy lifting and carrying .

One Christmas time I had been taken to the Circus by my mother. It was held in an enormous indoor exhibition complex called Bingley Halls. The circus tent had been erected in the largest arena. It meant everyone was spared the cold and wet weather but the wind that would have frozen us as we queued to get into the Big Top was now not blowing away the smells of the circus animals.

Even though I was used to horses and smog, the smell of lion, tiger and elephant could put you off your ice cream even if you were single-minded to enjoy it. So I was in a sulky mood when my school cap fell off and disappeared below the tiered seating. I was sent to rescue it by my mother who was tired of my peevish behaviour. But the world beneath the seats was dark, forbidding, scary and dirty.

I squeezed past the others sitting in our row, climbed to the back of the seating block and went down the outside stairs. The nearer to the ground I got so the sounds from the circus ring faded. When I reached the bottom of the steps, with the noise of the performance dimmed I searched for a way under the tiers of seating. I eventually found a small door, opened it and went in. It was like stepping through the mirror into an Alice in wonderland world but this one was dark, dank and fearsome. Mouldy straw was strewn on the ground and there was a glutting smell of cold muck aggravated by the close anonymity of the crowd sitting above: stale sweat, cheap perfume, candyfloss and elephant dung. I inched forward once my eyes had adjusted to the scanty pencils of light from above. I saw my cap and bent down to snatch it. Just then there was a roar from the crowd. I looked up. With the primitive open seating I could see all the audiences legs and above. There were rows upon rows of schoolboy knobbly knees and their mother's flannelette-clad legs and nether regions. One pair of ugly female legs captivated me: they were blue, veined and varicose. As I looked at them they slowly opened. As I saw there were no underclothes further up an elephant trumpeted loudly in the ring. It was like some hideous animal opening its jaws tempting me to become its prey. I had had enough. I scampered away back to the safety. But it had a lasting impression on me.

I didn't like Birmingham's underworld on my own and was glad to get back to civilisation and the comfort of my mother's custody, smells and all.

There were other things that frightened a young lad like me about Birmingham. My doctor father was called to a road accident one night. He came back pale and shaking and when he told me why I had nightmares. He had attended the scene of the accident and found himself alone in a deserted street.

He saw there was a body in the gutter so he went over to offer assistance or certify death. He tried to turn the body over by lifting one shoulder but the head had become severed and it rolled away down the street before he could react. Movement in a dead body is unnerving no matter how prepared you are as I would find out later when I trained as a doctor. All alone that night it shook his confidence. Birmingham was a scary place as a young and cosseted boy.

Now for the first time, as a new undergraduate, I had a city at my disposal. But it was a relatively tame city by modern day standards and I was feather-bedded. Birmingham now is a frenetic, cosmopolitan, rapidly-changing conurbation. Then it was still an industrial monolith. Heavy industry predominated. The city buildings were sooty and dark, the streets filled with lorries and busses and deserted during the day and night.

There was no such thing as a youth culture – everything was geared up to the adult world (the clothes, the food, the leisure activities). So now, back in the city as a teenager, as a young man entering dental school, I was now doing what generations had done before me – learning to become a clone of our elders and betters. Everything about the setup then was about making us conform, teaching us how to be like every professional person had been for all known time. But there were straws of change blowing in the Brummie wind.

At least we didn't have conscription. That was something previous groups had endured. Unlike my father's generation we didn't fear being called up to fight for our country. My doctor father had played his part in all that but not as a fighter. His job was to do the medicals on young men who had been called up. He had to sort out the malingerers.

Many boys of my age would try to get out of going to war. They feigned illness so doctors like my dad put them through a tough medical to weed out the fakers. But it was often an easy job to do.

One day a young lad came for his call-up medical wearing a borrowed truss. His ruptured friend had lent it to him so he could avoid having to go and fight in Egypt. He came in wearing the truss and when he was naked he proudly showed it off to my father saying, 'There, I have a hernia, I'm wearing a truss so I can't go and fight in the desert'.

My father replied,' Anyone who can wear a truss upside down can ride a camel. Cairo here you come'. Our generation were spared that humiliation.

Our cohort of undergraduates was among the last to be moulded into clones of our predecessors. Yes, we were more casually dressed, had longer hair and were interested in modern things. But our teachers were still battling to graduate dental replicas from the old school however much we tried to rebel, and they usually succeeded. When we left dental school we were pretty indistinguishable from previous generations. But the seeds of change were already sown and germinating.

The world of dentistry was changing. At that time everyone stood up: the dentist, the nurse, the patient if you found a particularly sensitive nerve with the drill. When we graduated patients would be lucky if the dentist even looked up from his seated position.

Going was the shoddy dentistry of old when dentists thought an autoclave was a motorway in Germany not a modern method of sterilisation. Soon dental nurses would stop applauding when a dentist got a tooth out in one piece, cheering when it was the correct tooth or marching round the surgery chanting 'hail the conquering hero' when the dentist did the injection and the extraction in the right order.

Also soon to be banished were the old dental occupational diseases: chip syringe eye (repetitive winking caused by air blowing back from a hand-held rubber dust blower), extractor's wrist (limpness through overuse) and dentist's hip (one hand resting on the hip to relieve back pain). If you got all three it could take a dentist hours to walk home though the red light district of town.

Dentistry was just emerging from the Dark Ages. We scoffed at some of the primitive materials and techniques used not that long before. Vulcanite was an obsolete rubber used to make the gums of dentures. The teeth were made of porcelain and made the falsies sound like castanets when they chattered in the cold.

We encountered vulcanite now and again when elderly edentulous patients came in for a modern replacement. The problem with it was it didn't retain its life-like qualities for long. The owners of a set made from it were doomed to look increasingly artificial themselves as their teeth lost any original naturalness.

Seeping in Steradent (a caustic solution of denture cleaner popular at the time) accelerated the deterioration. It was commonplace in those days for the elderly toothless to sleep with a glass of this potent brew by their bedside, working its magic as they slept. Unfortunately, with cleanliness came artifice. But it could also be dangerous stuff.

A relative of mine was a publican who drank more than he sold over the bar. He too slumbered beside his teeth in a glass of Steradent. But one night he awoke with a raging thirst and he drained the glass before he realised what he was drinking. So toxic was the denture cleaner fluid that for the rest of his life he had to attend hospital to have his gullet regularly stretched. No wonder the Vulcanite dentures surrendered their good looks to it in the name of hygiene.

Many of the materials we used when I trained were echoes of a bygone age. Before the invention of modern medicaments, dentists relied on chemicals to treat teeth because they smelled powerful, the theory being the nastier the substance the more potent it was. Oil of cloves, Oil of Wintergreen and camphor all featured in our materia medica, even though we now know they quietly killed off the germs and human flesh in equal measure.

We gaily filled teeth with lashings of mercury amalgam, even though many previous generations of dentists had gone quietly mad with exposure to the volatile, toxic metal. And we stuffed all sorts of noxious concoctions into bone, cavities and tooth sockets blissfully unaware that the cancer-provoking liquors we were applying were seeping all over the body to come to light years later.

The equipment we learnt on and used was actually very old-fashioned or was a tarted-up version of what dentists had been using for centuries. Admittedly the dental school was 'state of the art' as it had been equipped from new. So the dental chairs, the chair-side equipment and the cabinetry were superficially very modern.

Under most of the stylish exteriors beat a sclerotic heart of old. The dental chairs were modernised versions of the ancient 'sit up and beg' barber-style dental arrangement – patients sat up and dentists peered over their shoulder to treat the teeth. But when we graduated many of us found that the dental equipment in general practice, hospital and school dental surgeries still harked back to the dark ages.

Some of the kit we learnt on was soon to become obsolete. Much of the equipment to give general anaesthetics (commonly known as 'gas') in dentistry would soon disappear. It gradually dawned on governing bodies what a terrible risk to patients it was to let dentists put people to sleep in high street surgeries.

What was tolerated then in x-ray practice was not long to be endured – so powerful were the x-ray machines that we used to study teeth that they fogged the photographic films in the cameras of holiday-makers landing at the airport twenty miles away. What they did to the patients and us operators may never be known, but not long after better techniques came in, like very sensitive x-ray film and machines that didn't leak so badly.

The instruments we used in our hands were both ancient and modern. Many of the surgical tools were virtually unchanged from the early days of the barber-surgeons: the forceps, chisels, bone rongeurs and mallets.

The power tools were new and evolving rapidly. There were new-fangled air-driven drills and some micro-motor engines for hand pieces. But we still relied heavily on slow, old-fashioned drills that were mechanically driven and not long evolved from the belt drives of the 1960s. Again, many of us went out to practice dentistry and stepped back remarkably little when we went to work in what passed as commonplace dental setups in surgeries throughout the area. Even now those days come back to haunt me. I recently went to the British museum in London and was shocked to find the equipment I worked on when I graduated in 1972 labelled as 'a fine example of Victorian dental engineering'.

It wasn't just the individual materials and tools of the trade that were different. Dental treatment was actually in short supply so people queued to get an appointment or went on a waiting list. Cosmetic dentistry was a term of derision; there were so few dentists that no-one would have time to spend fussing over what were seen as fripperies, like what teeth looked like. And life was simpler then: if you wanted a nice smile the dentist would offer you orthodontics (teeth straightening with braces); nowadays dentists might just use Botox but your smile will never be quite the same again. Back when I trained the National Health Service dentist's job was to patch up the function of the nation's mouths not waste time making them look good. So the private sector cornered that market even though it had a small list of enhancements to offer.

Even then, dentists never strayed outside the mouth; it would have been unheard of, even shocking, for dentists to concern themselves with facial lines and wrinkles let alone dare to treat them with Botox. You could get struck off the dental register for less than that.

Dentists didn't spend all their time preserving the dentition. Taking teeth out was a large part of the job, and replacing real teeth with artificial ones was an essential skill. Nowadays extracting teeth, even one, is a last resort. I suspect today's dentist wouldn't know how to do what we had to, take out all some poor soul's teeth and fit an immediate set of full plastic teeth in one sitting (the patient, not the dentist). No, the dental world of the late sixties/early seventies was a different one from the one we have today.

One thing hasn't changed – the handwriting of dentists. Like doctors, dentists have always been known for their poor handwriting. It is something dental schools have never tackled successfully. They never will now as dentists rarely have to put pen to paper; everything is done on a computer. My dentist at home fell foul of his own bad handwriting. He'd been invited to speak to the local mother's union. He chose 'extractions' but his handwriting was so bad the chairwoman misread it as 'sex actions'. Tickets for the session went like hot cakes. Just before the event the dentist's wife was stopped by the chairwoman in the street. 'We're looking forward to his talk very much. He must be an expert'.

His wife was scathing. 'He's no expert. The first time he did it he fell off his stool and the second time he broke it off at the root'. Some good came of it. His mother's union patients flossed harder to save him lifting heavy scaling instruments.

6

Our place in the evolution of the dental world was far ahead of us when we mustered for our introductory lecture. Although we were dental students and destined to spend most of our undergraduate days at the dental school in the city centre, the preclinical year was spent on the main university campus, in the medical school. It was at one end next to the big teaching hospital in Birmingham, The Queen Elizabeth Hospital (The QE to everyone familiar with it). There medical students did their clinical training after their preclinical two years. Some of us also went there in our clinical years to study medicine and surgery related to dentistry. But that was to come.

The dental school was five miles from the medical school as the crow flies. Not many crows would have bothered to make the journey into town. Crows don't have teeth so they don't seek dental treatment. The Dental School was a barren place devoid of trees, shrubs or plant matter. The poor birds might have found a nice high vantage point on a low building but they wouldn't be able to build a nest or find a quiet branch to snooze on. And the dental school was so tall, the winds so gale force most of the time that the crows would have found landing there like doing it on an aircraft carrier in the Atlantic. No, a crow with any sense would prefer to stay at the medical school; it was on the main university campus, a rambling lawn-filled place where everyone had room to roam and there were lots of trees.

The front door of the medical school was easy to find. The building itself was art-deco and there was a big flight of white stone steps up to the dark metal framed thick glass doors. It took some effort to open a door even when there was no wind. If it was blowy, you could spend a long time trying to get in or out. But that day it was easy with all the students rushing to the first lectures of the term. I guessed some of them were contemporary students of mine but it wasn't until I got into the lecture theatre that I saw who were my fellow second year colleagues. I had travelled there from Mrs Bostock's with Leo.

The majority of dental and medical students started their course in year two. It does seem bizarre to miss out year one at university and I can't pretend that I was so brilliant they bumped me up a year. It was a simpler explanation and mundane as most of us were in the same boat. You only started in year one if you hadn't done the right A level exams. The norm was to go to dental school with the right combination of subjects in my case biology, physics and chemistry. Any other permutation relegated you to a year of studying the correct subjects but at university not at school.

So in the lecture theatre that day most of us were new to university. There were a few who had been there a year and passed their first Bachelor of Dental

Surgery examination, now joining the majority as second year students.

The lecture theatre where we all met for the first time was a museum piece itself. The benches were made of dark wood, there was a blackboard on the wall and the lecturer's area was a large laboratory-style bench raised up on a small platform with a lectern at one end and a sink at the other.

At the back of the room was an antiquated projection device. It was dark green enamelled metal and had a tall chimney. We later learnt that it was so old that it relied on an obsolete bulb. The bulb burned so hot it needed to cool off every twenty minutes. While it was on the chimney drew off the fumes and smoke in a losing battle.

There were old canvas blinds on the window which looked out onto a quadrangle at the back of the medical school. Across the way were the QE hospital wards.

As my dental year assembled in that lecture theatre we behaved like the strangers we were. We all realised these were our colleagues for the next few years so we had to be as sociable as our personalities would allow. Some came in groups and were obviously well acquainted already. I thought they must be old school friends but they turned out to be living in halls of residence so they had already started to form social groups. There was a lot of raucous bravado as these gangs took up prime positions on the benches – mainly at the back where they could fool around, laugh loudly and ruffle the hair of the hapless students in the row in front.

The rest of us were loners or in pairs, the ones who were living at home or in digs. We sat strategically, not too close to anybody else but not entirely on our own. It was a bit like men at a gent's urinal. There are unwritten codes of behaviour there. You can't stand too close or you'll be mistaken for a pervert. But you don't want to pee entirely alone or people will think you have something to hide. The same rules applied in the lecture theatre. The loners were spaced out at first but that all changed as the benches filled up. Our personal spaces were all compromised as more people squeezed in till we were in a state of forced intimacy. That led to our first introductions.

'Can I shit here?'

I looked up and it was a fellow newcomer.

'Pardon' was all I could manage, not sure whether I had heard him correctly or not.

'Can I shit down next to you? Is this space taken?'

'Of course, please do' was all I could say rather embarrassed that I had misheard what he said, especially as he seemed to have a speech impediment not a warped sense of humour.

He offered his hand.

'Woodcock'

Again I found myself saying 'Pardon'.

'William Woodcock, that's my name'.

'Oh, yes, my name's Ray and this is Leo'. He shook Leo's hand and we immediately ran out of conversation. I tried to think of something to say. All I could muster was: 'You straight from school?'

'No' he said, 'I came from my digs this morning. Oh, I see what you mean – yes, this is my first day at university. Took the right A levels so here I am'.

Pretending to look around the room, I had a surreptitious peek at William. He looked about the same age as me but dressed as if he were middle aged. He had on a three piece tweed suit, a shirt and tie with an old-fashioned detachable collar fastened on by studs. I knew the score because I had had to wear the same wretched apparatus at school when we paraded for Cadet afternoon in our ex-second world war RAF uniforms. But there William was wearing it voluntarily.

He also had a short back-and-sides haircut. My hair was unfashionably short compared to many of the Beatle-style haircuts of our colleagues but his was extreme. He also used some sort of greasy hair dressing reminiscent of my grandfather. He had a flower in his button hole and he wore a fob watch in his waistcoat. His brown brogue shoes were highly polished and he sported a monocle in one eye. He was a living anachronism but he seemed oblivious.

The rest of the year were remarkably homogeneous. Most wore casual clothes and had scruffy long hair grown wild in the last weeks of the pre-university holidays. About a third of them were girls and they were smarter. There was one black face, no-one with a disability and most sounded as though they had been to private schools. Yes, although we tried hard enough we were from common stock so it would not be too hard a job for our teachers to turn us into well-conformed dentists much like the generations before.

Suddenly a small door opened in the back wall of the lecture theatre beside the blackboard and a tall freckled white-coated man strode in. This was the first of many encounters we would have with Dr

Brockley Whins, senior lecturer in oral surgery and man about the clinic. He looked extremely confident as you'd expect from a surgeon, even a dental surgeon. This was a bone of contention we were not aware of at the time but which would loom in my later career choice.

Dentistry incorporated a number of sub-specialties. For each part of the mouth there was a body of expertise and a distinct group of experts. The fillers and crowners of teeth were in Conservation (Cons for short), the makers of false teeth were in Prosthetics. Gums were what people in Periodontics did and children's mouths were looked after in Children's Dentistry and Orthodontics (the fitters of braces to straighten crooked dentitions). Oral Pathologists looked after bits of the mouth that were discarded, Radiologists X-rayed what remained. In those days the Oral Surgeon was the self-appointed king of the castle.

Oral surgery thought it was a cut above the rest of dentistry. Partly it was because it was the goriest specialty; you can't extract teeth without spilling a little bit of blood and you can't dig out wisdom teeth without hacking off large chunks of bone. Oral surgeons undoubtedly measured their status on their ability to make onlookers nauseated. But they also claimed to be superior because they almost all had to have a medical degree as well.

A medical degree gave the dentist free passage into the general hospital ward and the casualty department. Because dentists claimed trauma to the mouth as part of their territory, they inevitably got involved in sorting damage to the wider face and head. To be able to work alongside the face, the brain and adjacent damaged bodily structures, and the medical/surgical specialties also claiming territorial rights, the dentist with a medical degree suddenly possessed the rites of passage into the bigger world outside dentistry. That sometimes went to their heads.

Dr Whins' head had been turned by his double qualification. We all guessed that on the day and it was confirmed later when we got to know him more. It gave him confidence that others lacked. He dared to stray into areas outside the mouth and be involved in treating more serious 'dental 'diseases like mouth cancer. Dr Whins and his medical colleagues would find themselves in demand in the dental school if a dental patient dared to have a non-dental problem, for example a pregnant woman going into labour or someone with a medical condition presenting with a toothache. 'Call Brockley Whins' was music to his ears rather like the summons of a star witness in a high profile crown court case. He relished the status and basked in the glory. His dental colleagues resented it all but had to bite their tongues in case they would need him to bail them out one day.

Brockley was not shy in exploiting what he saw as his star status in the dental school. He made a bee line for attractive women in the place whether nurses, students or junior staff dentists. He thought himself a real Casanova and played it to the full. This was resented by his professional colleagues and most of the women he came into contact with. He was too flighty by half, supposedly loving and leaving his 'conquests' far too casually. He left a trail of broken hearts but that seemed to fluff up his ego more. No, he was about the only person in the dental school who thought that he was a heroic figure.

Philanderers like Dr Whins used to have their evil way with their current conquest in the residential quarters of the nearby general hospital. Senior oral surgeons like him were able to use bedrooms for professional reasons, for example if they had to stay overnight after a difficult operation or if they had to be on call when a complex case was being treated on the wards.

He could even have a bedroom over lunchtime to allow him to change clothes if he needed to wear his academic gown for a ceremony in the lecture theatre, like when a visiting academic dignitary was honoured with a degree. He abused this facility so much that the domestic staff complained they had to change the bed sheets every time after him even though it was a lunchtime booking.

He eventually got his comeuppance. Usually he came back after a lunchtime session with his latest conquest beaming with pride and strutting about to everyone's annoyance. This day, and I witnessed it myself, his mouth was encircled by a bright purple colouring like he was a circus clown that had gorged on messy chocolate. He looked so smug that no-one told him what he looked like until he saw his first afternoon patient. Meanwhile he had been in the canteen, in the library and even had a walk around town looking at the shops. He thought that everyone staring at him was just his pure animal magnetism.

Only when the patient pointed out his purple beard did he look in the mirror. Aghast he dashed off to the men's room in horror to wash it off. But it was indelible. He feigned illness and with his head wrapped in a scarf he slunk off home. Later we discovered that his paramour had been treated by the local venereology clinic for a mild infection of her external genitalia. Her clinician had painted the area liberally with the purple-staining antiseptic Gentian Violet. At least it cured Dr Whins' cold sores though he didn't see it in that light. And he went right off oral sex.

That was all in the future. For now, Dr Whins looked very much the part, the first real dental teacher we had seen and he was talking to us as brand new recruits in his, no, our profession. We hung on his every word. He was tall and good looking, in a blonde-haired, freckled faced way, just as you would expect an ambitious surgeon to be. Though junior by staff standards, he seemed typecast as the thrusting surgeon dentist: big hands making confident sweeping gestures, speaking from memory, making eye contact especially with the attractive girls in the audience.

He was able to do this because the introductory lecture was the most tedious duty a junior academic like him had to do. And because he had been volunteered to do it, he learnt all the banal details so he could use the opportunity to ogle the crumpet, play the dental matinee idol and once again enjoy the sound of his own voice.

The new students listened to every word as of course we were hearing it for the first time. 'Most important time of your lives.....privilege for you all to be here.....getting in was the easy bit....five years of damn hard work.....the rewards are worth it....'. And on he went. So engrossed in his performance was he (and so intent in making a mental note of which girl he preferred and what she might let him do) that he almost forgot the important bit, about where we were to be tomorrow, and what we would be doing. In fact, even though we were dental students and this was the dental school, we would spend our first year at the medical school. So it was hello dental school and goodbye. For a year.

After Dr Whins had finished a second lecturer stood up at the lectern. She was an attractive woman in a white coat, a bit stern I thought but worth listening to as we weren't going anywhere yet. When we found out what she was talking about we all paid close attention. Dr Whins introduced her: 'This is Dr Janet Fourchette and she is going to talk about sex'. You could have heard a pinafore drop.

As she expounded on her topic I whispered to Leo, 'Cor, this is what university is all about'. Apparently her job was to warn us of the sexual world we were entering after our sheltered school days. She then went off the boil a bit by wasting time on some anthropological details about the sexual nature of tribes in Africa and I began to lose interest as she compared the mating habits of the shrew with the three toed sloth.

Then she suddenly brought us all back to attention. 'You have to understand different sexual practices. Don't be confused by thinking you know all the possible permutations: man with woman, woman with woman, man with man and so on. There are many other variations.' We were all ears.

She shocked us with the next question: 'Has anyone here ever had sex with a ghost?' We all looked around the lecture theatre to see if anyone was going to be foolish enough to volunteer. I couldn't see anybody so was a bit disconcerted when the front rows turned and looked in my direction. I couldn't understand why until I saw that Leo had his hand up. 'Put your bloody hand down you fool' I urged; 'Don't call attention to yourself'. But it was too late.

Doctor Fourchette had seen Leo's hand and was urging him on. 'Come down to the front of the theatre, son, and tell us about your experiences.' And he was actually going down, pushing past people in the row and walking down the gangway. I make an effort to distance myself from him telling William 'He just sat next to me, I don't really know the lad actually….'

People were tittering as he was walking down. He got onto the stage and Dr Fourchette said, 'Young man, it's very brave of you to come down and tell us all here about your experiences having sex with a ghost.' And Leo, looking sheepish said, 'I'm sorry miss. I think I've wasted your time. I thought you said 'a goat'.'

My new classmate was turning out to be a liability.

7

In the preclinical years dental students didn't go within spitting distance of real live patients. Nowadays that seems old fashioned. Today's dental student starts seeing patients from day one even though they don't lay a finger on them - they are dental novices just like we were. But nowadays they start learning and practicing communication skills, though they are like eunuchs talking about sex: all mouth and trousers because when it comes to sorting the dental problem the patients came in for, the novice student eventually has to hand over to a real dentist. For anything other than a mouth rinse the first and second year students of today are as impotent as we were. Now they talk a lot about doing dentistry but perform just as little as us which seems to me to rub salt into the wound. Back in the old days we didn't bother with communication. We cut up the dead.

We were introduced to death in our first few weeks. We were given tours of the body store to show us how the dead were made ready for dissection. The curator took us round in groups. My group were keen to see inside the refrigerator drawers so he opened them up for us one at a time and showed us the body inside. The first one looked very peaceful as if he had died when he was asleep.

'This man died a peaceful death' the curator told us. 'Rigor mortis has preserved that demeanour so we can see it even now, months later'.

We were all rather reassured by what we saw. We relaxed as we moved on to the next drawer. But this inhabitant was entirely different. The body had a terrified look on its face and we all recoiled at the fear registered on the cold, dead features.

'What happened here?' we asked.

'This person must have died in agony' he said. 'The face says it all, frozen for all time by the rigor mortis.' We were all much less happy at this turn of events.

The third draw was a relief. The cadaver's face was wreathed in smiles, his hands were open in a gesture of amazement and he looked altogether much happier. We were eager to hear what circumstances had been preserved in rigor mortis this time.

The curator solved the mystery. 'This man was killed by lightening – but he thought he was having his photograph taken'.

Within months we were no longer spectators. We would have to start cutting up these bodies. Nowadays, cutting up dead people is passé, but we did it warily. It was one of the great mysteries we reckoned we would be initiated into as student dentists along with sex, drinking alcohol, staying up all night and being rude. It was supposed to be one of the things that separated us from non-medical mortals, the fact that we stuck scalpels into people, chopped up dead bodies and looked inside where ordinary people never saw. We were told we were privileged, but in reality we were scared.

What would happen if we fainted when we went into the dissections room? What if a body was not really dead and sat up screaming when we got chopping? Would we vomit at the smell, run amok at the sights, lose our nerve when cutting something important? We couldn't wait to find out, but we dreaded it at the same time.

The dissection room was high up in the medical school. Nowadays it would be in the basement for it doesn't matter to today's student or cadaver whether the light is natural or artificial. But when we started dental school natural light was thought to be best, so is was done in cavernous, high-ceilinged rooms in the roof where the tiles were replaced by frosted glass.

It was bright the entire day. And all that light was essential because the embalming process rendered the human flesh a uniform pale colour. So only under the brightest light could you distinguish muscle from nerve, artery from vein, liver from kidney. When you peeled back the skin, it all looked like a confusing mess of bits of string, gristle, blobs and grey lumps of matter. And if you touched anything you recoiled in horror because it was all so hard – the preservative solidified all the tissue so where there had been soft, warm, coloured flesh, everything was now stiff, smelly and colourless.

On our first morning we waited outside the doors of the dissecting room acting like this sort of thing happened every day. We were louder, ruder and more boisterous than we had been up to now in our short dental career. It was pure bravado masking our anxiety. And it was made worse because the doors had glass windows in but they were opaque. In the distance through the glass we could see ghostly figures moving about. I stupidly wondered if these might be the bodies getting back onto the dissecting tables after a night off. It made me chuckle, which made me look even more nervous, so I reined in my emotions and joined the others as we gradually fell silent. Soon no-one spoke as we waited for the doors to be opened. The tension mounted. You could have cut the atmosphere with any one of the scalpels we had in our little canvas roll-up pouches.

We gasped in unison as the doors opened and we went in, trying to saunter both bravely and gingerly. We must have looked like a collection of patients with bizarre nerve diseases that made us walk like Barbary apes. But eventually I was in and with the others I clung to the small area just inside the door like ships blown against a harbour wall by a strong wind. And while we were marooned there, we took in all the sights. And there were many.

The whole room was lavatorial. It was mostly tiled white. Along one wall was a row of large deep porcelain sinks with strange taps; they had long handles that stuck out to left and right. There were some stainless-steel sinks almost the size of baths. The other walls were shiny, hard and white, and every sound was amplified and echoed. But the sounds were not important. The sights were.

Along one wall was a shelf holding various glass jars. Most were the size of the bottles that sweets were displayed in in confectionery shops. But they didn't contain toffee or anything else like sweetmeat. The jars were filled with tea-coloured liquid in which wallowed hunks of something in various shapes and sizes. They looked just like assorted misshapen pickles in jars. We soon realised they were human organs, preserved in formalin for who knows how long, destined to hang around functionless and ownerless long after their dead proprietor had been interred, incomplete but finally laid to rest.

In one corner there were four articulated skeletons. The grim row of bones were dangling shoulder to shoulder like the remnants of a good mass hanging when the bodies had been left to rot down. The skulls grinned, cheerfully but foolishly unaware that they had little to smile about. And down the middle of the room were the dissecting tables, each with a body already ravaged by the scavenger dental students congregated around it like a carrion-eaters get-together.

I now had a good look at the bodies. Most were clothed in muslin like mummies from a horror film. They lay stiff and obscured one to a table. Many tables were unattended, lonely and unvisited until some group of nomadic student dissectors were to take up residence around them. Some tables were industrious with dissection, a hive of activity around a lifeless centre of attention. Here, bodies were in various stages of dissection. Some were hardly touched, perhaps with an incision opening up the abdomen like an adjourned operation. Others were ravaged like the abandoned carcass of a Christmas turkey after a greedy onslaught. Moth-eaten arms drooped over the table edges, fingers pointing while tendons dangled down, unwelcome bracelets of the dead. Some faces looked intact on one side but the other was nibbled away and exposed, with an eyeball prominent and incongruously staring out, unseen and waiting to be punctured and dismantled.

We waited by the door, a group of lost sheep, anticipating being herded somewhere by someone. We all had on newly-starched white coats. You could tell we were novices by the newness of our clothes. The more experienced, professional dissectors ahead of us wore the scars of their battles with the corpse with casual pride – stains of many colours, bits of flesh, biro jottings, all showing the experience and couldn't-care-less attitude of our senior colleagues. And we couldn't wait to be that casual, that nonchalant. Within weeks we were old hands at dissection.

William, Leo and I were assigned the same body. After a hesitant start we became blasé, even jaded. One of us would hack away at the flesh, another would read out from the instruction book, the third would stare into space, go wandering about the room to see what was going on with the others or fidget with debris on the table.

Leo was a prize fidget especially while William was dissecting. William was too slow for Leo, too meticulous, too fussy. Leo would flick more and more debris further and further until one day he miscued and flicked a large piece of preserved human flesh into William's mouth as he yawned. He was so engrossed in his dissection that he reflexly chewed it like it was a welcome morsel of food. But the formalin preservative soon burnt his mouth and he spat it out, right at the feet of the member of staff supervising the dissection. He got a grade D minus for that.

Leo also couldn't resist playing jokes on William. Once he drove him mad for days by secreting a length of spaghetti in between a set of complex dissected nerves on our specimen. William went berserk at his digs in the evening searching in the anatomy textbook in vain for this newly-discovered nerve. Eventually he asked the demonstrator who peered at it, lifted it up gingerly with a pair of tweezers, recognised its pasta parenthood and gave him another D minus.

Finally William got his revenge. He followed Leo into the student union toilets and filled the toilet bowl with intestines from our cadaver. When the supposed results of his bowel movement were pointed out to him, Leo was convinced he had just passed his internal organs and rushed to the medical centre. He was devastated they didn't believe a word of it. William deserved an A plus for that and we got him one when the dissection room staff heard how Leo had got his comeuppance. That's justice for you.

After months of dissection we all grew very bored with the physical task so many of us read ahead trying to find the clinical relevance of the mysteries we were uncovering and what each bit of the body did. While we were dissecting the anal canal one girl in our group found a condition that affected live patients – pruritis ani, intense itching of what lay people call the 'ring piece'. But she had not had a classic education including Latin so she pronounced it to us all as 'Pruritis Annie'. We all laughed at her ignorance (at least the classical scholars among us) and forever more she was known as Pruritis Annie. She never lived it down. And people would call after her as she walked down the corridor, 'Pruritis Annie get your bum'.

8

You don't expect to be physically assaulted as a dentist but it happened to me some years after I qualified. It just goes to show how much what you do as an undergraduate can come back to haunt you.

I was at a conference in Cardiff and I noticed a young woman across the auditorium. I recognised her. She was an ordinary university student when I was a dental student and I'd fitted my very first gold crown into her mouth, and it was the very first crown that she'd received. Ah, the pleasures of treating your first patients and the thrill of breaking a duck with each and every new dental procedure.

I hadn't seen her since those far off undergraduate days so during the coffee break I pushed through the crowd of delegates to find her. I went over to her. It was a good 20 years after I'd met her last and she was standing there with all her business colleagues having coffee. I said to her, 'I recognise that mouth. 20 years ago I put something in there which made us both very happy.' She slapped me so hard my ears were ringing for the rest of the conference. What a waste of a conference fee.

It brought it all back though, how dental students gradually learn the ropes, what sort of patients you study on and how you progress from the simple to the more complex.

The thing about undergraduates is that, as soon as you learn a little bit of medicine or dentistry, you are convinced you're the bee's knees – you imagine you're an expert. And you're dying to try out even the simplest things that you've learnt.

When I was a dental student the first thing we studied was how to examine the mouth including removing the patient's full dentures. You can't just pull them straight out. You have to swivel them around on their horizontal axis because they're wider at the back than they are at the front. If you pulled them straight out the lips would expand and you'd be left with flabby chops.

I really got the hang of all this and I was out one day at lunchtime walking when I came across a little crowd of people outside a bank. I was curious so I pushed my way through and there was an old lady on the floor obviously unconscious. Apparently she'd collapsed. Her shopping basket was upside down and her possessions were all over the pavement. I thought this was my ideal opportunity to show off my new prowess so I said to the crowd, 'I think we need to take her teeth out.'

Some clown said, 'Why's that?'

I had to think quickly – I said, 'In case she chokes on her teeth.'

A bystander piped up, 'Oh, yes, marvellous to have an expert on the spot.' I was encouraged so I knelt down. That was my first mistake because there was one of her eggs from the basket under my knee so I felt a squelching as I lowered myself to the ground. It threw me but I quickly recovered and thought, 'No, I've got to prove a point here.'

I looked in her mouth and yes, sure enough, I could see false teeth. So I prised open her mouth put my hand in and started to pull. Now the problem was they were stuck very firmly. I hadn't ever come across this before at dental school. I started pulling really hard. And as I tugged at the gnashers her head started bobbing back and forwards like a rag doll.

The crowd was starting to get restless now with a, 'Well, what's happening, why aren't the teeth coming out?' I was getting more desperate. Then she opened her eyes and she looked at me.

Her expression was a mixture of surprise and anger. Then the bitch bit me on the fingers. I let out an expletive. The crowd weren't impressed at all. 'Oh, tut tut. A professional person,' and the like. Which made me even more determined to pull the teeth out. So I pulled and pulled and pulled and pulled. Suddenly they shot out with me holding on to them.

They came out so precipitously that I fell back onto the pavement. I scrambled to my feet as fast as I could brandishing the false teeth in my right hand, showing off to the crowd like a matador with the fallen bull's ear. But the crown weren't ecstatic as I expected. They were aghast.

I looked up and saw what the problem was: they weren't a full set of teeth, they were partial dentures, the type that are held into the mouth by real teeth. I'd pulled out the partial dentures with the real teeth attached. What I had in my hand was a mess of plastic and real teeth roots and all. Blood was dripping down my hand.

By this time the old woman had begun to recover. There was blood and foam spluttering out of her mouth and she was trying to get to her feet. I ran off. Just before I turned the corner to get away, I heard somebody shout out, 'Let's hope he's not at bloody dental school'. That brought me down to earth.

After you swot the basic sciences and pass your first professional exam you begin to learn dentistry proper. But that professional exam is a big hurdle.

Dentists and medics had to clear two sets of obstacles to get on at university. One set was the University exams, familiar to anyone who has studied in what's known as tertiary education. To leave University with a degree most people have to pass a final examination. These are held during the last term of the last year. They are the culmination of the traditional UK three year course of study. When I trained the final exams were a test of the whole of the curriculum. Nowadays you can sit and pass modules along the way. It makes life easier as you don't bet your whole degree on one set of examinations. But vocational degrees like mine had an additional layer of scrutiny.

There was also a set of so-called professional exams to pass. As I was studying for the degree of Bachelor of Dental Surgery, we had to pass second BDS, third BDS, fourth and fifth BDS as well as finals. First BDS only troubled a small group of undergraduates who didn't have the precise subjects when they left school; this exam, sat after a year at university, made sure all students studying for dentistry started out with the same baseline knowledge. After that, to progress in your dental studies you had to pass each and every one of the professional exams as well as passing all the other university and departmental exams set during the course. It meant us medics and dentists worked harder than many other undergraduates.

It didn't mean that we were completely dedicated to our studies. Nowadays students have to earn their bed and board as well as pay their fees and pass their exams. They don't have time for many extra-curricular activities. But we belonged to a golden generation. We were the beneficiaries of the UK welfare state where University fees were paid for us and we got a free grant to live on. All we had to do was to pass the exams and not get expelled for bad behaviour. Many of us sailed close to the wind on that last one – misbehaving was almost regarded as compulsory for undergraduates but the medics and dentists were comparatively well behaved. And as the years went by we had more to lose.

We were not like ordinary undergraduates. Not only did we have more exams but our course was also longer by about three years. This had an effect on many aspects of our lives. The friendships we forged early on in our student careers were often broken as we carried on our academic studies while our colleagues graduated and went on to work. So we often started sharing living accommodation with early acquaintances but ended up with dental colleagues as our early cohabitees moved away.

Our course was also far more practical than the average undergraduate. Even the medics didn't do as much as us. Soon after we started attending the dental school full time we began to acquire the technical skills that would see us through a dental career. This all started in laboratories on the top floor of the dental school.

Even though there were only fifty of us in the year, the laboratory seemed immense. It occupied one wing of the school. There were rows and rows of wide benches topped with dark hard wood (nowadays it would be synthetic plastic material). The benches had sinks with unusually tall taps, Bunsen burners plugged in to gas outlets and small shelves filled with jars and tubs of materials and chemicals. But dominating the benches were rows of belt-driven drill engines sticking up in the air and looking like miniature cranes lying idle on a vast area of dockland. It was a busy vista and we would be occupied here for many months.

This was called Optech one (Optech two was later when we learnt more advanced techniques). Here we would learn the basic dental proficiencies and master the materials and the tools of the trade. And what we would learn about was dominated by the major disease we were fighting – tooth decay. Dental caries (the major cause of tooth loss when I was training) was perhaps the commonest disease experienced by most people in Western Society after the common cold.

It seemed no-one escaped it. If you looked in the mouth of the average United Kingdom resident in the late 1960s you would either see untreated dental decay or the repair work that had resulted from it. It was said by our teachers that the British mouth was a give-away if you believed in the class system. Poor people had untreated decayed teeth if they had any at all. Many would be toothless.

The upper classes often had a dentition well restored with yellow gold even though the teeth were misaligned and unkempt. Years later there was an episode of the Simpsons comedy cartoon series that depicted the British ruling classes in a disreputable book called 'The Book of British Smiles'. In that tome Prince Charles, the heir to the throne, was depicted a buck-toothed chinless wonder. The myth still survives – Americans regard British teeth as pitiable and for many years dental decay contributed to that myth. We sweated for hours learning how to patch up after decay had done its worst.

Nowadays dental decay eats away small holes in the teeth and the modern restorative dentist's work reflects that. Ours was a massive hole-filling job. Dental decay was epidemic. There was even a condition called rampant caries in which the disease ravaged the whole mouth like a forest fire fanned by a hurricane. The tinder for the destruction was bacterial slime on the tooth surface and the fuel was refined sugar. So rampant caries was found in the sweet-eaters. We were a nation of those back then. The more sweets you ate, the worse was the decay.

I worked for a while as a new dentist in a well-known local confectionary factory where workers could help themselves from the production line. The dental service had been set up in the medical centre to fight the losing battle against rampant caries in the workers. It was like painting the Forth Bridge and failing – we couldn't drill and fill their teeth fast enough.

So we dental students were in the mass market as far as fillings were concerned. Everything we learnt was about big scale: filling materials had to be able to cope with large holes, instruments were designed for remote and deep working, drills came with larger and larger tips, probes came in longer and longer sizes, tooth substance could be replaced in greater and greater proportions.

If we lost the battle to save teeth, we also learnt how to replace them with plastic full dentures, metal partial dentures or at least preserve the root. We would fill it in the gum and prop up a crown on the submerged wreckage either singly or in a row as a bridge. There was no restorative challenge we couldn't rise to and we were armed with a cupboard-full of materials to match.

Mastering materials played a big part in our training. No, this is not training to be a tailor. 'Materials' here refers to all the liquids, solids and gases we use to treat dental disease. Take a decayed tooth. Once you have drilled out all the decay and the tooth is saveable you need to fill the hole with something that will stand up to everyday action in the oral cavity: hot liquids, grazing, grinding, gnawing, chomping, chewing gum, chattering in the cold. It's a lot to ask of a restorative material.

Some materials are better than others in some situations. Metal fillings can be tough but heat up quickly in hot liquids and can make the tooth sensitive. Hard fillings can resist firm pressure but shatter if suddenly stressed. White fillings can look nice at the front of the mouth but might not stand any masticatory action.

The dental student has to learn what substance to use in what circumstance and how to get it to perform the way it should. You may need to insert a strong filling in a sensitive tooth so you need to put a protective lining at the bottom of the hole. You need to be able to manipulate both materials to get the satisfactory finished restoration. All this has to be learnt from scratch.

Early on in your practical dental training pops up the issue of manual dexterity. To be able to carry out intricate procedures in the confined space of a mouth takes some doing. Getting into dental school requires brains not good hands, though nowadays they make an attempt to check that prospective dental students aren't completely cack-handed. But it was assumed that if you weren't dextrous before you went to dental school they could teach you. And the teaching consisted of getting you to learn the skills on artificial teeth in the Optech laboratory.

It didn't stop with the filling materials. We learnt to make plaster of Paris models, cast metal, carve wax, set plastic teeth, bend wire for orthodontic braces, fire porcelain for crowns, sharpen steel instruments, handle scalpels, tie stitches, mix impression materials, solder copper, weld steel, stick things to other things, chemically-cure plastics and manipulate cements.

We also learnt to make false teeth in the laboratory. These are rare nowadays but were commonplace when we trained especially in the elderly. They were rendered edentulous one by one or had the lot out at one sitting, for example to increase their wedding prospects if they were women (The Glasgow Dowry). Whatever the path to falsies we mastered them from impression to fit.

Impressions of the toothless gums were tricky as some of the ridges were flabby. Metal trays were chosen to sit loosely over the upper and lower jaws and impression material was inserted before it hardened thus capturing the state of the gums. Compo (our term for the impression material) was solid when cold, soft when warm. It was stored in a hot water bath. The trick was to fill the tray and let it cool enough not to burn the patient's mouth but not to let it harden too much so the impression was blunted. There was a lot of hand-burning and lip-singeing getting it right.

We made try-in dentures in the lab from plastic teeth and wax gums. One of Leo's patients sneezed violently during the try-in stage and expelled the teeth like buck shot. It was an art to get it all completed without mishap.

William, Leo and I were on the same bench and we kept together as a small clique. We got to know the whole bench and we spent the days laughing and joking as we mastered the essential technical skills. The staff were friendly enough but they eventually demanded perfection. We had to get it all right before we could go on the clinic so our work was scrutinised closely and regularly.

Sometimes the banter got out of control. One lunchtime William Woodcock went rummaging in the lab store cupboard. He found a large nearly full bottle of pure alcohol; it was used as a solvent to clean adhesive from metal trays. He put it inside his jacket and hid it in his bench-side locker. He explained how he had made his find and showed it to us craftily when we came back after lunch. All afternoon he would regularly fill a glass beaker from this bottle; he offered it around but no-one wanted to get drunk except him. He thought he could hold his liquor.

The first sign he had underestimated the strength of the brew was when he got a loud bout of hiccups. They were heard across the lab and members of staff who came over to ask what was wrong had to be fobbed off with ever increasing fanciful tales. William blamed the dental school canteen rissoles. Then he got more boisterous. He started laughing hysterically at the slightest thing. When he snapped off a tooth he guffawed. When he drilled into the bench he creased up and when he forgot to light his Bunsen burner after turning it on, he was poleaxed when there was a loud explosion from the pooled gas in the sink.

He became intolerable about teatime. He suddenly decided he was going to recite his favourite drinking party piece despite vigorous objections from the rest of the lab. In it he usually pretended to get drunk as he was telling it. This time he was drunk for real. He lurched to his feet and started.

'I had a number bottles of whiskey and was told by my wife to empty the contents down the sink or else. I said I would and proceeded with this unpleasant task. I withdrew the cork from the first bottle and poured it down the sink, with the exception of one glass, which I drank'.

William slurped another half beaker of his lethal spirit and continued.

'I then withdrew the cork from the next bottle and likewise with it, with the exception of one glass, which I drank.' He spilled most of this one.

'I extracted the cork from the third bottle and poured the glass down the sink, which I drank. 'He raised the glass so fast most of the contents went over his shoulder. But he pressed on.

'I pulled the cork from the fourth bottle down the sink and poured the bottle down the glass, which I drank.' He took a swig from the empty glass, looked at it quizzically, bent down and refilled it spilling most of it onto the bench.

'I pulled the sink out the next glass and poured the cork down the bottle. Then I corked the sink with the glass, bottled the drink and drank the pour. When I had everything empty, I steadied the house with one hand, counted the glasses, corks, bottles, and sinks with the other, which was 29 and as the houses came by I counted them again.' He sat down triumphantly to a smattering of applause. He slumped forwards and fell asleep on his arms snoring loudly.

We all heaved a sigh of relief and got on with our lab work. His gentle snoring suddenly got louder, he choked, awoke, stood up confused and carried on. A groan went round the room.

'Finally, I had all the houses in one bottle, which I drank. I'm not half as think as you drunk I am. I fool so feelish I don't know who is me and the drunker I stand here the longer I get. I'm not under the affluence of incohol as some tinkle peep I am.' He sat down, opened his mouth and belched loudly. The neat alcohol fumes shot across his lit Bunsen, ignited and engulfed Leo's head. There was a smell of burning hair. William fell on the floor and slept until going home time. Leo's eyebrows regrew much redder than his hair and extremely curly. But no-one bore a grudge and it was never mentioned again.

Leo continued to be a practical joker in the lab and he spotted an opportunity to have some fun at William's expense when we experimented with a new dental adhesive. Adhesives were going to be big in our dental careers. Up to that point fillings had to be secured in the teeth by mechanical means, for example by putting them in deep and undercut cavities. This was destructive of tooth tissue so the possibility of gluing in fillings was welcomed. We had to get to know the new adhesives quickly and we tried them out in the lab. But they were unpredictable at that stage of their evolution.

The adhesives we played with were unreliable setters. Get the mixture right and it would set firmly and in a given time. Get it wrong and you might get a very rapid setting or none at all. Us students tended to err on the side of rapid as a non-setting glue was no good. It was a question of getting the most rapid set you could handle at any given dental opportunity.

Leo wanted to test the power of the new material's adhesiveness on William. When our hapless colleague was over at the sink Leo smeared his seat with a liberal helping of the adhesive mixed to a rapid set. Once William had sat down we all waited for the experiment to unfold. It did quicker than we had anticipated.

'This cavity is very poor Mr Woodcock'. It was a particularly nasty member of staff and he was waiving about an extracted tooth that William had been drilling.

'I'll correct it sir' William limply said.

'No you won't' and with that the tutor walked over to the window, hauled it open and threw the tooth out. It sailed gracefully down towards the pavement.

William was up like a shot to try to save his handiwork but the seat went with him glued as it was to his coat. The weight of it made him stumble and he knocked over the cruel staff member who in turn grabbed the window sill as he fell. The shock of William falling chair and all caused the window to slam down shut on the fingers of the tutor.

'Sorry' said William lamely.

'D minus' said the member of staff but he wasn't able to mark William's card at all what with his pulverised fingers. William got away with that one. Leo wasn't so lucky. He was grassed to William as the culprit for the gluing and the pair didn't talk for weeks. It meant we were able to get on with our work in peace so every cloud has a silver amalgam lining.

We also mixed medicaments, made up pastes and dressings, learnt to thread wire, attach steel brackets to teeth, turn screws to make plastic palates widen on demand, use rubber sheets to isolate teeth from saliva, take and develop x-rays, service drills and motors, look after hand instruments and operate all sorts of machines (centrifuges, dental chairs, suction apparatus, lighting, lamps to cure light-sensitive agents, clamps, dental stools to sit on, spirit lamps to heat things up in, volatile sprays to cool things down). And that was before we ever saw a patient.

9

By the time we were sent on to the clinic we could do a great deal. Occasionally we had practised on each other; more often we had rehearsed on artificial mouths nowadays called 'phantom heads'. In our day they didn't bother to pretend they were real mouths – just the odd plastic or extracted tooth set in a block of plaster of Paris would do. As we got nearer to treating genuine patients the simulations got more lifelike: rows of teeth placed in upper and lower plaster jaws and mounted on a clamp in mid-air where a human mouth would be. We had to imagine the person round the ghostly spectre and begin to treat this less as simulated therapy more a dress rehearsal for the actual thing.

We looked forward to our first encounter with a live patient with mounting dread as we sat out our days in the laboratory. But there soon loomed one of the most important rites of passage every dental student must pass – the mouth mirror.

Almost everyone who has been to the dentist will have been on the business end of a mouth mirror. It's a small round metallic mirror about the size of a large coin and it is set at an angle on the end of a silvered handle. It's a miniature of those gadgets the security guards use to look for bombs under cars.

It is still used widely today in spite of the introduction of endoscopes (miniature cameras able to go anywhere in the body through any orifice). So the mouth mirror is ubiquitous in dentistry. It is used to see round corners so allowing the dentist to look in every nook and cranny in the mouth without getting his or her head in the way of the light. But it takes some mastering.

For a start, the surface area of the mouth mirror is very small. To see a lot you have to keep it on the move like an eyeball constantly peering about. Secondly it is in a hostile environment as the mouth is warm, moist and in motion. What with the saliva, hot breath and spray from the drill, it is difficult to keep clear the field of view. Windscreen wipers and centrifugal spinning have all been used to keep the mirror dry but none have ever been perfected so there is a constant wiping that accompanies the use in the clinic. But finally, the real rite of passage is being able to see the mouth as a mirror image and do all the necessary manipulations upside down. It takes some doing but eventually, often quite suddenly, a dental student gets the hang of it. We first made this transition in the laboratory but we eventually had to make that leap from artifice to human flesh.

Before you meet a patient in your own right as their dentist (even though you are a student) you must look the part. And many dental students will tell you that it is a rite of passage when they put on their professional white coat for the first time. It may just be a garment made of humble cotton or synthetics but the dental white coat assumes a significance way beyond its simple cut or its utilitarian styling. You as the wearer change when you button it up, but others see the difference as well.

Suddenly people begin to take you seriously including yourself. It is supposed to have that effect on the patient but others feel the influence: nurses suddenly see you though they may still hold you in contempt (only when you qualify and have power does that change); reception staff in the dental school treat you differently but more as a nuisance because you will cause them endless frustration as a student and can only answer back when you graduate; and members of staff who can exert more control over you once you are branded as clinical and therefore fair game for their power games. Yes, a lot changes when you don the uniform of the embryo dentist. But it is only when you actually play out your new role that life changes.

They say you never forget your first patient but that's not entirely true. It's everything about your first encounter with him or her that sticks. The encounter is the stuff of drama. You are in your new costume (the white tunic coat), you are on an unfamiliar stage (the student clinic), in an alien setting (surrounded by dental equipment) and you are about to meet your first serious challenger (the patient). No wonder you are nervous. There is palpable tension in the air as you and your colleagues wait like a row of greyhounds in their racing traps.

In the name of efficiency and crowd control, the layout of the student dental clinics was what we now call 'open plan'. Down each side of the floor was a series of mini dental surgeries (with chairs facing the windows) separated by solid wooden and Formica baffles.

These pretend walls were only shoulder high. If you were sat in the dental chair it looked as though you were in a small dental suite. Up at head level, for all those standing, it was like an enormous battery-hen shed for humans with rows of students and staff intent on their own treatment domains. Down at patient level it was relatively calm; they could stare out the window with most of the action going on behind them and out of eye line. Up at operator head level it was frenetic.

In and out of these two virtual worlds did the students and staff oscillate – you could have a quiet word in your patient's ear then straighten up and summon help with just a flick of the neck. But you had to get the patient into the chair and that was a palaver in its own right especially the first time you did it.

Even the system of communication between reception and your treatment cubicle seemed to be designed to add to the drama. On the top of each cubicle dividing wall was a series of lights. When your patient arrived in the reception area the receptionist could indicate that happy status by changing the colour of your lights. The lights would already have shown you were ready and waiting and when the patient was in the chair a further colour change would declare this even happier stage. A final colour combination would announce when your patient had departed.

So your treatment progress was marked, even controlled by the lighting system. We students eventually invested a degree of control in the system it never deserved but to us it seemed to exercise domination way beyond its authority. We felt slaves to the system just like later when I qualified and had the same hate-hate relationship with my electronic pager.

Still, on the first day we came under the rule of the lights these thoughts had not developed. We stared at the lights until the desired (yet feared) colour change happened and then we were off to get our first patient.

We soon became blasé about it all. After the first patient experience we quickly got the hang of the ballet-with-lights. It was soon commonplace and every day. We then had other things to worry about as more rites of passage loomed, for example our first local anaesthetic injection on a live patient.

Rites of passage come thick and fast when you start on the clinic and none looms more so than your first inferior dental block local anaesthetic. As most people come to learn, teeth are sensitive. They have a complex nerve supply and can become painful if injured. Toothache is dreaded by people who have ever experienced it and the dentist suddenly becomes your friend if you suffer from it. And if treatment involves interfering with teeth (like for example drilling out dental decay or extraction) that can be a painful encounter for the patient. So the dentist must be an expert in pain relief and the local anaesthetic becomes a stock in trade. You can be put to sleep with a general anaesthetic to save you the pain of treatment but that is a bit extreme when only the tooth itself need be numbed. It is much safer and less complicated.

Local anaesthetics are administered by injection. Even the inept dentist has to get the anaesthetic near the tooth but William Woodcock didn't even manage that the first time. He trembled so much as he advanced on the patient that the needle jammed into the tip of the patient's nose. By then he was an expert bluffer.

He calmly put the syringe down and explained to the patient,' Just testing a new anaesthetic. When the nose is numb I'll risk the rest'.

The poor tame patient believed him and submitted to more attempts at an injection interspersed by 'waiting time'. At the end of the long session the patient went home still with toothache but with a number of numb patches of skin around his mouth. Eventually even William mastered getting the anaesthetic where it needed to go.

The anaesthetic fluid is deposited near to the tooth where it soaks into the pain-carrying nerves and stops them transmitting that noxious stimulus for as long as it lasts. For many teeth (especially in the upper jaw) all you have to do is to inject though the gum next to the tooth and the thin and porous bone holding the tooth will let the anaesthetic soak through unhindered.

Some teeth, especially in the lower jaw, are set in thicker bone. This infiltration technique won't work so the dentist has to block the nerve where it surfaces from the bone internally. The inferior dental block is the commonest example of this therapeutic trick and it is a rite of passage for dental students to this day. Dental students and patients never quite get used to it.

You need a bit of dental anatomy to understand the inferior dental block (IDB). Open your mouth, take a hand and grasp the opposite cheek between the thumb and fingers so your fingers are on the outside and your thumb on the inside. Now push the hand further back. Your thumb will bump up against a bit of bone under the flesh. This is the ascending ramus of the lower jaw. The dentist giving the injection does what you have done and then sticks a long needle past the thumbnail because the nerve he or she is after is back in there. As it will be dawning on you, this is done blind as the dentist can only surmise where the nerve is not see it. That's what makes the IDB such a trial for the patient and a rite of passage for the dental student. It is uncomfortable because the needle has to be long and the injection deep to find its target; it is nerve-racking for the novice dentists because it is such an act of faith. And it can go wrong unless done well.

Because it is a difficult procedure the IDB doesn't always go to plan. The nerve the dentist is after may elude the injection so the required numbness isn't forthcoming. This can happen if the anatomy varies and you never know when that is going to happen. Or the dentist may miss the mark by going too deep or not deep enough. This is a common error made by the beginner.

It happened to William Woodcock on his third try at an IDB. He waited a long time for the injection to work testing the patient's lip sensation tediously until he had to get a member of staff to give a successful second injection. That was delayed because the patient in the next door cubicle had collapsed when he'd tried to get up from the chair.

The fuss made getting the fallen patient sorted caused a hiatus in the clinic and the staff were unavailable for the duration. But William's anger and frustration at the delay soon turned to embarrassment.

It eventually emerged that William's first failed attempt at an IDB was the cause of the entire ruckus. The patient in the next cubicle had fallen to the floor because of William's poor technique. He had gone far too deep with his long needle which had poked out through his own patient's cheek. He had pressed the plunger only to shower his neighbour's patient and the anaesthetic had found its way down his collar soaking in and taking out the vital nerve that controlled walking (that was William's expert opinion because of his poor grasp of anatomy. There is no such nerve). The patient had complained about getting wet, tried to get out of the chair and his legs had given way (not because of an aberrant nerve, more likely the wet floor). William got a D assessment for his IDB which I thought was uncharitable.

A second rite of passage for us dental students came soon after our first local anaesthetic injections: the first extraction. A new twist on an old expression applies to the first extraction by a dental student: *this will hurt you more than it hurts me.* And that's what makes it harder for the novice extractor – you know you are inflicting pain and discomfort but you have to do it anyway. And you appreciate your bungling first steps in this technique are adding to the poor patient's suffering but you have to put those feelings aside. This is where a further rite of passage rears its ugly head.

The dental student goes through that invisible barrier and becomes a little colder, a little less empathic, a bit more psychopathic when the first tooth is removed under an inferior dental block. You have to acquire this distancing from the patient to be able to function as a dentist and it is a significant step in your development. Rest assured is painful for the dental student as well.

Taking a tooth out is not what it seems. For a start the tooth is not pulled but pushed. The removal of teeth is often called *pulling* by lay people but you won't get far as a dentist if you try to pull most teeth out. They are too well anchored for that to work. Only teeth that are loose come out by pulling as with a child's deciduous tooth helped on its way by a tug on a string. Most teeth need to be pushed. But it is a special sort of push. Teeth are extracted using dental forceps and they work because the tips of their blades are sharp. Applying the beaks of the forceps to a tooth and pushing along the root into the gum allows the sharp beaks to sever the tooth's attachment and at the same time to wedge open the gum. The loosened tooth is then levered out using the pliar-like design of the forceps.

So you don't pull the tooth, you push it. And you don't have to use too much force either. The leverage you can get because of the forceps handles and angled beaks allows even the weakest dentist to remove all but the most firmly rooted teeth. So whatever your strength you soon become good at taking teeth out as long as you used the correct extracting technique. Within weeks of our first extraction we were almost taking teeth out with our eyes shut just like our patients. We needed to be that blasé as many of our National Health Service patients needed more extractions than fillings.

We learnt mainly on patients from the National Health Service. But some of our patients had been in the private sector so we were fascinated to learn what it was like up that end of the market place. One of my patients had been to the private sector, and she told me all about it. She'd been to a clinic in Harley Street. But when she sat down in the elegant waiting room she suddenly felt this overwhelming desire to break wind.

She told me, 'It was a really posh place, brochures on the table, high class decorations and potted plants'.

She felt impending doom and embarrassment; she was so desperate to fart but mortified to do it in such exalted surroundings. So she decided that she'd do something to cover the noise, disguise what she was going to do hoping that nobody would notice. So as she farted she bent down and ostentatiously picked up the leaflets making a big fuss scrutinising them. Unfortunately, the receptionist heard her bodily exclamation and my patient became completely flustered.

She said, 'I'm terribly sorry; I do apologise.'

The receptionist took it all in her stride and said, 'Don't worry. When you hear the prices you'll shit yourself.'

No, it was the NHS for us and most of our patients, and that meant free density but also student dentistry – oral care without the frills.

We used to do everything for ourselves as students including develop x-rays. Not only did we do the dentistry but we did the ancillary chores that would be done for us by nurses radiographers, technicians and the like when we qualified. But in the meantime we did everything: from set up our kit and ready the surgery for treatment through bringing in the patient; carrying out all the chair side nursing duties like mixing cements and wiping the patients dribble to escorting them out (sometimes actually carrying them after a particularly gruelling session); and making their follow-up appointments and clearing up the surgery. Sometimes the clearing up was a herculean task if vomit was included and it wasn't always the patient's. Developing x-rays was a regular thing.

An x-ray taken of a tooth is quite a small object. They were in a sealed packet and were about the size of a business card. The film packet would be placed inside the mouth behind the teeth and an x-ray beam shone though from the outside. The film would then be taken to be developed so the x-ray could be viewed. There were developing rooms on each of the clinics as taking x-rays was a common procedure for dentists. Teeth are highly mineralised so you can't see inside them without the aid of an x-ray. The film was sensitive to the rays sprayed by the x-ray machine but it was also affected by light. So the films had to be developed in the specially darkened rooms. It was quite a rigmarole going in to do the business.

Armed with your exposed x-ray packet you would excuse yourself from the patient and head for the developing room nearest to your treatment cubicle. You often had to develop the film there and then as the x-ray result was pertinent to the treatment you were carrying out. For example if you were doing a root filling, where the nerve of the tooth was removed and the space filled right down to the tip of the root. You had to be able to measure how accurate you were in filing and cleaning the deepest part of the root in case you went too far and caused post-operative toothache through over-enthusiastic boring.

Occasionally you would take an x-ray and develop it at your leisure between patient appointments. But it usually had to be done in a hurry so there was a sense of urgency to the dark-room routine.

Assuming the room was unoccupied you could go in and claim occupation by switching on the warning light. This illuminated a sign over the door saying 'in use'. It also switched the interior light over from a normal bulb to a safe-light which was harmless to x-ray film. It meant you were bathed in a warm red glow and were safe from being disturbed. No-one was supposed to come in when the warning light was on in case they let in light as they opened the door and fogged your x-ray film. It was a precious bit of privacy in the crowded world of a student teaching dental clinic. Anyway, you had a rigid procedure to be getting on with so you welcomed the solitude.

What a fussy palaver it all was developing your x-ray. Like a professional chef, first you had to make sure all the ingredients and equipment were to hand. If you stood with your back to the door, there before you was a draining board that led to a deep sink. In it were four tall, square tanks. Two had lids on, the first and the third from the left. The first tank was the developer. Next was water to rinse. This was followed by the fixer tank, and again the last tank was pure water for washing. The film had to be dipped in the developer for a certain time, then washed, then fixed in the third tank, then finally washed. It was then ready to look at in daylight even though it was wet.

Drying off in air over the next hour or so would allow the films to be stored in paper packets or mounted onto clear plastic viewing sheets, all to be stored in the patient notes. But if you were in the middle of a root filling you wanted the wet films on a hanger beside the patient to do your measurement. But you couldn't just take your time with the tank-hopping.

How long the x-ray film dwelled in the various tanks was temperature dependent. This was another aspect of the dark room. The tanks were kept at a constant temperature. There was a thermometer in the developer which showed what temperature it was at and you timed the dipping process according to that reading. The warmer the liquid, the shorter was the immersion time. And it was a knife edge procedure – a few degrees warmer and the film had to be dunked for a much shorter time. There was even a huge clockwork timer with an alarm to make sure you followed the sequence meticulously. Get it wrong and the film was ruined. No wonder you had to concentrate on what you were doing.

That was why I was too distracted to react one day when someone slipped into the room behind me when I was well into the dipping and rinsing cycle. I was completely absorbed in the process – the clock was ticking, the timings were tight, there were a number of x-rays on the metal rack and my hands were wet. I had to be especially careful as I didn't know whether the wetness was developer or fixer. Handle the film with hands wet with the wrong chemical and it would be as ruined as if I had flung open the door and welcomed in the midday sun. Having an unexpected passenger threw me completely.

Whomever it was slipped in behind me and snuggled up. I tried to move away but my forward space was blocked by the sink. I was sandwiched between my new pillion passenger and the bench and they had their arms either side of me. I was completely boxed in. And the perpetrator was pressing me hard from behind. Not knowing who they were was very disconcerting. Not a word was said by my new dark room assistant. I was about to ask them to declare their identity when their hands began to wander down towards my trousers.

The timer alarm suddenly shrilled and made me jump. I regained a little composure and transferred the rack of films onwards in their developing journey. Then I caught a whiff of female perfume and my companion blew gently into my ear. In spite of myself and my predicament, I began to relax and enjoy the experience. I decided to concentrate on making sure at least the x-rays turned out satisfactorily even if I didn't. I was interested to see what developed.

You must understand that to an inexperienced boy like me who has lead a sheltered life, this sort of encounter is high on the dream agenda but seldom realised. I was transfixed by the welcomeness of it but frozen by the reality. Here I was being seduced in a dark room by someone who was almost certainly female (I could make out the required contours through my back), wore attractive perfume and, what's more, seemed to find me irresistible. It was a fantasy come true. I had never thought of sex and danger before and the mixture was heady. And it was working much lower down as well.

It never occurred to me to wonder who might take this bold risk. I assumed, as most boys of my age and experience did, that it was par for the course for such a high status in-the-making person as me to attract this sort of adulation. After all we had come into dentistry partly because it was a prestige calling. I naïvely assumed I was getting what was rightfully mine early. So I went with the flow. And something else was about to flow if she kept on agitating it with her hands as she was doing now, playing the front of my trousers like she was frantically fingering a piano accordion.

She now had me well cornered. She had loosened my trousers and they fell round my ankles. I was about to enter heaven when she grabbed hold of my manhood and pulled it up abruptly. The tip caught under the sharp lip of the sink and I yelped. Any tumescence quickly deflated. I stood on tip-toe to lift my wedding tackle free of the lip and it ended over the edge of the sink. It was now wedged between the developing tank and the sink. I had to strain to stay on my toes unless I wanted to be castrated.

Somehow this was a cue for her to disappear. She turned away and opened the door. I immediately lost my balance and fell back. Determined to catch the culprit I flung open the door and gave chase. But the trousers round my ankle made we waddle.

I needn't have bothered to chase her. Whoever she was, by the time I got out of the developing room she had melted into a rather large crowd of my fellow students and nurses from the clinic. I felt a proper Charlie. The feeling was total when they said in unison: 'So that's what she meant by a penguin'. It had been a set-up all along. The x-rays I was developing were ruined, my reputation was floored, and from that day forward I found the smell of x-ray developer brought on instant impotence.

One big difference between dentistry and medicine when you're learning is that you do things in dentistry: you do fillings, you make false teeth, take real teeth out and so on. They're concrete entities and you can have them assessed. So all through the course we were plagued with the need to judge what we had done, graded A, B, C and D. Each item had to be scored. Whereas when I trained as a medic because you're doing less concrete matters (counselling, interviewing people, the laying on of hands) it isn't so easy to evaluate these procedures, to stand in judgement of what or how we were doing. As a dental student you were very aware that you had to get everything right.

So when I made my first full upper and lower denture I went through all the aspects of the dentures I'd made to make sure they were correct before I called the tutor over to get a mark.

I said, 'Clench your teeth together; is the bite all right?'

The patient nodded his head.

I said, 'Run your tongue round the teeth; do they feel about right.'

Yes he nodded his head.

I said, 'Smile and have a look in the mirror; do they look OK?'

He nodded his head.

Eventually I thought I'd got everything right; the shape, the whiteness, the bite, the chew, and all those sort of things. In the end I called over the tutor. All he said to the patient was, 'How are the dentures?'

The patient said, 'They're marvellous' and with each S he whistled surprisingly loudly. 'Absolutely wonderful [whistle].' Because the articulation was wrong, because the teeth had been badly set up, he couldn't speak properly. And as the tutor was giving me a big fat D, this patient kept on and on. 'They're [whistle] superb. Absolutely superb. [Whistle]. I've never had dentures [whistle] like them.' And I thought to myself, 'You [whistle] silly [whistle] sod.'

There were other ways we differed from the ordinary undergraduate. Early on we were introduced to representatives from commercial companies that sell dentist's equipment. This is one of the things that distinguishes doctors from dentists. When dentists graduate they immediately practice their craft. So from day one they have to acquire equipment and materials. Dentists become economically active as soon as they set up shop. This may be delayed if they work as a junior to an established dentist but they must still understand the harsh economic truths of the business of dentistry. So our training included lessons in the trade side of the profession.

One day on the clinic we were introduced to the commercial representative. Doctors see many reps in their practicing lives especially if in general practice. The drug rep (a representative from the pharmaceutical industry) is forever trying to get in to see the general practitioner to try to persuade him or her to prescribe the latest drug produced by the employing company. It's a constant battle between reps eager to peddle their wares and the doctors keen to avoid the hard sell. The reps get a much warmer welcome from dentists.

The ones that call on dentists are from a different industry. They are not trying to push pharmaceuticals. They are more interested in the chairs the patients sit on, the stools the dentist perches on and the rest of the surgery furniture whatever it does. Almost everything that is needed for dentistry is sold commercially so there is legitimate business to be done between the commercial traveller and the dental practitioner. It doesn't always work out well.

Long after I graduated as a dentist I went to work in a practice owned by two friends from dental school. Paul Cateswell was the serious one who did all the business side and Gilbert Littlethorpe was the more easy going. He was easy going with everyone: the nurses, the patients, the junior dentists but especially the commercial reps. He would spend hours listening to their patter and usually had to agree to buy something to get rid of them. He didn't have the heart to turn a garrulous rep away empty-handed. But he ended up with a lot of useless equipment. One particularly successful salesman re-equipped his surgery with what he convinced Gilbert was the latest technology. It was the dental light to die for.

Most patient mouths were lit for treatment purposes by a single beam from a powerful light mounted on an arm rather like a standard lamp. But Gilbert ended up with a series of spotlights on the ceiling, all aimed where the patients mouth should be. Unlike a conventional light they were immovable. If the dentist needed to peer into the mouth close up, a standard dental light would let you move it to one side so you could shine the light from another angle. Not this new arrangement. The lights were fixed and focussed brightly on the mouth area.

When Gilbert bent over to scrutinise closely his latest oral masterpiece his head would eclipse the light like a giant heavenly body. Added to this his eyes had been dimmed by the glare of so many spotlights and his pupils were tightly constricted to keep out much of the brilliance. In the shade it was all too murky for him. To cap it all, his bald patch bore the brunt of the spotlights' intense beam when he leaned forward. He was half blind and had a blistered bald patch for his troubles. But he was convinced this was progress. What a rep that was.

So we undergraduates needed to be educated in the ways of the commercial representative if we were to be canny purchasers. So one day we were invited to scrutinise the latest rep to visit the dental school department of conservation.

What a cheeky blighter he turned out to be. Before he was even completely through the door he'd tipped a bucket of vomit on the floor. Everyone was aghast.

He said, 'Don't worry, folks. Today I've come to demonstrate the new miracle electric aspirator. I will suck up all the vomit with this new miracle electric aspirator and you will not see a smidgen of puke when I've finished.'

The head nurse said, with a wry grin on her face, 'It will be a miracle, we've had the electricity cut off.'

10

Dentistry is not the same as medicine. Being a dentist is not being a doctor for a small part of the body. There are different skill sets and the training reflects that. This is not always apparent to the lay person, or, indeed, to professional colleagues. Many doctors assume that dentists have it easier than them what with a shorter training course, a less complex apprenticeship, a smaller part of the body to know and a limited set of diseases and cures. But they are fundamentally different.

In fact dentistry is more like the branch of doctoring that is surgery. Anyone qualifying with a medical degree can go on to train as a physician or a surgeon (they may also go for pathology, radiology or one of the other less mainstream specialities). But the big difference is between being a physician and being a surgeon.

Physicians are philosophers. According to their rival surgical colleagues, physicians spend inordinate amounts of time pondering, thinking, investigating and experimenting with various drug regimes. Seldom do they do anything (or at least did anything – nowadays, physicians can and do do more, whether it is looking inside patients with endoscopes or using potent drugs or electrical stimuli and so on).

Surgeons, on the other hand, were always regarded as people who did things (operations) whether they were needed or not. That has now changed to a degree – these days surgeons use drugs and other interventions more. In fact surgeons and physicians are more alike than different nowadays. It was not so when I trained.

Thus it was between dentistry and medicine at undergraduate level. Medical students spend most of their student years watching plenty and doing very little. They only became more hands-on when they became senior, near to graduating. And then they got more involved helping practising doctors on the wards (by, for example, taking blood, assisting at operations, booking patients into hospital and running tests). It was only when medical students graduated and became new doctors that they started to acquire hands-on experience officially.

Dental students did far more as undergraduates. During their training they had to acquire and perfect a whole series of practical skills: examining teeth, taking teeth out, making crowns and dentures. This was because when they graduated they were expected to be able to carry out actual treatments as most went into clinical practice straight away. So they had to be able to function as real dentists from day one of their postgraduate life. Newly-graduated medics spent a year in supervised practice in hospitals before they could go out and look after patients on their own. Dentists went in at the deep end much sooner.

One of the practical skills dentists need to develop is how to fill teeth. So-called plastic materials were used to fashion fillings in the patient's mouth. The materials were not made of plastic; they were plastic in the sense that their shape was determined by the cavity they went into. If a tooth was decayed the hole left by the carious process would be shaped and finished using the dental drill. The defect would then be made up, the hole filled, using one of the plastic materials, for example silver amalgam for a weight-bearing chewing tooth, or silicate white filling for a front tooth that needed to be aesthetically passable. Nowadays the range of plastic materials has expanded and the quality of them has improved.

Amalgam and silicate, the two mainstay filling materials when I trained, were temperamental. They abhorred moisture so controlling the saliva in a patient's mouth was a constant battle. If the filling material was contaminated with patient spit it might not set properly or the filling might come loose after a short period of time. And these fillings were not the blandest of things. Amalgam was part mercury and in my day it was mixed by hand at the chair side. Silicate white filling needed a precise mix of liquid and powder and it set very quickly, faster if it was warm.

In complex cavities the shaping of the finished job demanded the placing of artificial walls against which to fashion the material so it set with smooth contours. This involved the fiddly placing of steel and clear plastic matrix bands, which themselves caused the gums to bleed and made moisture control even harder. It was all a juggling nightmare for us new dentists.

Other ways of restoring decayed or impaired teeth had been developed especially for teeth that were extensively damaged. Plastic fillings were only as good as the solid tooth surrounding them. Nowadays, modern plastic filling materials bind to the tooth so don't need so much support and can be used in larger holes. But then we were limited to small enclosed cavities for the narrow range of restorative options at our disposal at the chair side. But in a laboratory we learnt how to make more robust devices.

Crowns, bridges and inlays were made and used to restore more damaged teeth. Where a plastic filling was impracticable because there was too little tooth remaining to support it and give it something to survive in, we turned to the stronger materials of gold, porcelain and the like.

Gold had been used by our forefathers at the chair side as a plastic filling material in the same sort of cavities as mercury amalgam. It was soft gold and could be burnished or worked into the hole using pressure with hand instruments. It was only good for back teeth and it was harder to use. It was also expensive. But apart from burnished gold, fillings made from metal and ceramics had to be made away from the patient in a laboratory. So we spent a good deal of our undergraduate time learning this trade up in the laboratory.

Of course when we graduated and went into dental practice we wouldn't do this sort of back-room work for ourselves. We would employ our own technicians or contract with commercial laboratories for all that. But part of learning how to commission the work was to do an apprentiship undertaking the whole process, a bit like working our way from the factory floor to prepare for the boardroom in an engineering company. There was some chair side parts to the complex restorative work and we did all that in Optech two.

If a badly broken-down tooth is to be rebuilt using porcelain or metal there are a number of steps from start to finish. The tooth has to be prepared and shaped using drills. If a rigid material is to be placed in a tooth, the remaining tooth needs to be fashioned in such a way that the restoration slips in and out but can be secured permanently with cement when finally fitted.

The shaping of the receiving tooth substance is quite an art to master. Make it too easy for the crown or bridge to go in and it will equally easily drop out no matter how strong the cement. Get the insertion path too tight and the manufactured filling won't sit down properly. There was little room for manoeuvre in the process. And patients don't appreciate fillings that don't stay in or that don't bed down properly.

Stage one was to prepare the tooth to receive what was made in the laboratory and to allow it to stay in for as long as possible. Thus a high degree of accuracy in this early process was needed. Once the tooth had been prepared satisfactorily (and had been closely scrutinised by a dental tutor) the next stage was to take an impression. Rather like biting into a lump of cheese, the teeth were pressed into a soft material which set hard and retained the imprint of the teeth in minute detail. Again, these impression materials took some handling.

In the quest for the ideal impression material, dental scientists had looked at all sorts of possibilities. Most didn't meet the requirements: some were not accurate enough, some weren't up to the manipulation stresses of being manhandled into and out of the mouth, some were toxic, others were too sensitive to salivary contamination, others were just too costly. What we were left with was a small range of compromise materials.

One such material called Rubber Base was messy, clingy and stuck to everything it wasn't supposed to like bubble gum to human hair. It was accurate enough but it took a genius to get it right.

Silicone impression material was better but it needed two different types to be used simultaneously, one accurate and runny, the other rigid but inaccurate. It was a juggling act to get the two to work in unison but it was easier than Rubber Base.

There was a third alternative, the old fashioned way, which involved shaping copper rings to hug the teeth filled with a shellac-based material that needed melting in a Bunsen burner and an over-wash of plaster of Paris in a metal tray. It was very accurate but was too exasperating for us impatient youngsters. But somehow we got a good enough likeness of our prepared teeth, again inspected by out tutors before we could finally cart it off in triumph to the laboratory. Then the real fun started.

After the disciplines of the clinic, our time in the laboratory on Optech two was a chance to revert to our student type, a pack of raucous animals out for a collective good time. We were disinhibited and there was a lot of banter. Sure, we had to get on with serious work but it made life more tolerable if we were able to shout to each other, throw the odd soft missile and swop stories of our real or imagined social life outside the dental school. But even though our minds free-wheeled, our hands were busy making things.

We were fully occupied in the laboratory learning how to make crowns and bridges and we got bored at lunchtime. One day we're looking out the window and there were some workmen laying paving stones. We were watching them intensely when the foreman looked up and he said: 'Oi! Oi! What are you lot staring at?'

Leo was quick off the mark and answered back, 'Well, sir, we're in the same business as you, you know; we're into precision – putting things into exactly the right place.'

He added, 'We have to work to tolerances of a 1,000th of a millimetre.'

The Foreman looked up with contempt and said, '1,000th of a millimetre? That's no good for us. In our job you've got to be spot on.'

The mouth impression newly arrived in the laboratory had to be transformed into a dental restoration. This started with the casting. The impression was filled carefully with liquid plaster of Paris while simultaneously applying a vibrator to banish any air bubbles from the set plaster. Get a bubble in a critical area and it might be back to square one, down on the clinic once again straining to get another accurate impression. Impression materials could only be cast in plaster a set number of times before they would lose their precision and the crown made on the duff model would go nowhere near the intended tooth.

Next, if the filling was to be in metal, the cavity in the plaster teeth was filled with molten wax which was shaped and carved into the required form. Once approved by a tutor, the wax forerunner of the finished tooth renovation would be encased in strong stone material, the wax burned off and a casting machine used to replace the wax with metal. This would be finished and polished before fitting in the clinic, usually a couple of weeks after the impression had been taken, longer if there had been mishaps on the way. And those happed a lot especially in our first few months in the laboratory. Things often went wrong at the casting stage.

A centrifugal casting machine is used to transfer molten gold into the body of the restoration. You have to melt up gold until it is liquid using a blow torch, then you fling the gold down into the mould using centrifugal forces. This was a potentially dangerous procedure , using the centrifugal casting machine, especially if you over-wound it.

One memorable day we were all sat in the lab and William Woodcock, by now the course clown, was next door in the casting room winding up the centrifugal machine and we could hear every last movement he made. With every turn of the centrifuge spring more students would put away what they were working on and settle down to listen. The more he wound the more we concentrated because we knew he was over-winding the centrifuge.

Sure enough, all of a sudden, there was a 'Boing', a sort of nasty metallic springing sound, followed by a whoosh (like an arrow shooting through the air) then a loud wailing.

Poor old William.

He had indeed overwound the centrifuge. Gingerly he had poured the molten gold into the crucible and stood back. He released the catch and a blob of red hot metal shot down into the casting mould, broke through the bottom and sailed directly for his manhood inconveniently in line with the blistering molten missile. But he had some presence of mind and he was young enough to have keen reflexes.

He leaped out of the way with what for him was a super-human effort, something he had not done since he recklessly tried to put the shot on his last school sport's day. That had resulted in a minor rupture in his groin muscles. This time he got the full rupture. He had to leap out of the way of the golden missile with such exertion that two lumps came up at the back of his neck. And it took the local physiotherapy department three months to massage back down his testicles.

11

Community dental health was one of the small specialties that we studied. It concerned itself with the dental health of populations rather than individual patients. And one of its major successes had been the fluoridation of drinking water supplies in the Birmingham area (as well as in the North East of England).

Water fluoridation (the adjustment of fluoride levels in water supplies) is a safe, effective and economical means of preventing dental decay. It can halve the number of fillings, tooth loss and other resultant dental problems in the population served by the treated water or so we were told. Fluoride occurs naturally in almost every source of water in the United Kingdom. Fluoridation of water supplies involves the adjustment of the existing level of fluoride to one part per million where the existing level is lower. This level has been found to be optimal in terms of benefiting teeth. It had been known for more than 60 years that the natural presence of fluoride in drinking water at that optimal level reduces dental decay by about half.

This positive effect on dental decay was first shown in the North East of the United Kingdom during the Second World War in children who had been evacuated to the Lake District in the West of the country. It was spotted that children from the naturally fluoridated South Shields area had much healthier teeth than the local Cumbrian children. This led to a study of dental health in children in North Shields, where there were very low levels of fluoride in the water, and South Shields which showed that those south of the River Tyne had much less decay than similar children on the north bank, although the populations were otherwise much the same.

The issue of water fluoridation had not been entirely plain sailing. Although there had been much research showing that it was safe and effective, over the years there had been assertions - unsubstantiated by rigorous scientific investigation - that a whole range of undesirable side effects were associated with water fluoridation.

A small but very vocal group of people strongly opposed to water fluoridation had sprung up and they exercised the dental public health people regularly by attacking the intervention on every occasion, for example in the media and press. They became very active when water fluoridation was debated at public meetings. We dental students became involved in these public debates.

At the time I was a dental student there were very few people actively opposed to water fluoridation (so called fluorophobes). There were probably a handful of core activists in the United Kingdom, dozens of non-core and a few hundred fellow travellers. They operated as a loose network. There were ring-leaders (core fluorophobes as they were called), collections of core and non-core fluorophobes and a small army of sympathisers who become active when the issue becomes topical. We in the dental profession were convinced fluorophiles.

Who or what is a core fluorophobe, a non-core and a fellow traveller? Hard core fluorophobes were regarded as delusional about fluoride in drinking water. Less committed, non-core fluorophobes could see the merits of the antifluoridation case, were sympathetic to the cause, and were prepared to undertake some activity: they may distribute leaflets, turn out for meetings and be on the mailing list of antifluoridation organisations. Fellow travellers were regarded as floating voters who had been taken in by antifluoridation propaganda, either because they had been convinced by the arguments, or because the antifluoridation cause sat well with other beliefs they had (for example political).

We dental students were invited to attend a public meeting on water fluoridation to see the fluorophobes in full flight. We were skeptical that they even existed or that they had any particular axe to grind. We assumed the community health lecturers were making mountains out of molehills. We didn't see how an issue as clear cut as water fluoridation could cause the sort of fuss they promised us.

The fact that a public meeting was being held at all astounded us. We still didn't understand that an issue like adding fluoride to drinking water might have something to do with the democratic process. We were used to things being done to people by professionals without the need for a public debate. We were put right about this view so we reluctantly agreed to go and see democracy in action though we were mildly skeptical and exceedingly uninterested.

The meeting was held in the Cannon Hill Arts Centre, a modern complex of buildings devoted to the arts and which comprised galleries, workshops, rehearsal rooms and a theatre (where the meeting was scheduled). The building was so new and architecturally forward that it came as a shock when we arrived and saw the audience. Mind you, getting in wasn't easy. There was a picket line of protesting fluorophobes outside. Paradoxically many of the people there to protest against fluoride refused to cross the picket lines on principal. So some of our opponents were left stranded outside the meeting, hoist on their own petards.

A mixture of people were attending the meeting: students, retired people, men and women from all walks of life. Many of the audience were elderly people and I suppose it's because this is a personal issue for them. They remember the war and talk of bromide in the water and they get worried about *big brother* out to poison them and they are very keen on their water being *pure* as they see it (that is with no added fluoride). Many of the people against fluoride were elderly and had no teeth. The thought of some remote authority adding something to the water which wouldn't benefit them personally apparently used to set them alight.

When we got to the meeting and went inside there was an odd bunch of people who congregated apart from the main audience. These were the fluorophobes. They were older, dressed slightly oddly (with mismatched jackets and trousers/ skirts and tops, hats worn indoors, eyeglasses dangling on strings round their necks) and they had a furtive, paranoid look about them. Years later I would see this same group when I was a junior doctor, in psychiatric outpatients. For now there were two distinct groups in the room. We sat with the majority, a mixture of local dentists, us students and other pro-fluoridation people and unaffiliated members of the public. The phobes sat in a clique.

The meeting was chaired by a local councillor. She professed to be neutral about the issue but immediately peppered her introductions with loaded innuendos and sly allusions suggesting to the uninitiated that we were there to try Nazi war criminals rather than to discuss a public health issue. We were shocked at her early declaration of partiality. Our professor whispered that this was par for the course on these occasions and to watch her and her cronies and see how they played it out. It was pure theatre.

The Chair reluctantly introduced the first speaker, our professor of community dentistry. He had come to give the pro-fluoridation case though we assumed it was a forgone conclusion and that he would just have to give the audience a metaphorical pat on the head. We had heard all the evidence in our lectures and it seemed cut and dried to us. We yawned as we anticipated just another version of his standard lecture.

Professor Epididymis was uncharacteristically nervous. He tripped up as he mounted the stage, he dropped his notes before he could start to speak but most of all he made a considerable effort to avoid making eye contact with the small cabal of his sworn enemies. They did their utmost to stare him down. We were transfixed from the start.

Lecturers in medicine and dentistry tended to be a confident lot. As we were beginning to learn, part of the trick of being a successful medic or dentist was being able to bluff. Doctors and dentists often have to show leadership and decisiveness in the face of incomplete information. So our teachers were good at this especially when they were schooling us undergraduates. They were on firm ground with subservient ignoramuses like dental students. Not so this audience.

Unlike his normal self, professor Epididymis was halting, shifty, uncomfortable and almost inaudible. The case for fluoridation seemed weaker and he was almost apologetic presenting the topic. Rather than use his stature to bluster and bamboozle the audience (as he did with us in the dental school), he was apologetic and feeble. This was the first time we had seen feet of clay on one of our elders.

It didn't help that he was heckled. The fluorophobe section of the audience gave him a rough time. We students sat rigid in case the Professor thought it was us but nearly everyone in the room realized that only one section of the audience was unruly. They mumbled, hissed, even booed. The professor was not used to this and it showed. He cut short his lecture, sat down abruptly with a meek 'I rest my case' and his face relaxed with a look of intense relief. The chairman gave perfunctory thanks and then she introduced the main speaker for the opposition, a doctor Fergus Mousetit.

Doctor Mousetit was a middle-aged male with half-moon reading glasses. He took up a position beside a rack of test tubes on the table each containing straw-coloured liquid. He was dressed like an old-fashioned general medical practitioner: tweedy type three piece suit although has jacket slung over back of chair, doctor's bag meaningfully on the table in front of him. Next to the bag was a bathroom shower hose. I guessed this was some sort of fluid extractor or medicament applicator. Later it dawned on me he had meant to bring his stethoscope to bolster his image. Pity his poor wife back home trying to wash her hair with his stethoscope.

As he spoke he put his glasses on and off, sometimes speaking over the top of them. It was quite a performance but what struck me most was how confident he was. Compared to our own head of department, Dr Mousetit was expansive, relaxed, jovial, chatty and made piercing eye contact with whomever dared to look at him. I had been detailed to take notes so this is almost what he said.

'It's very satisfying this. Of course part of the Job, but I do this partly out of enjoyment and partly out of the sense of calling really, duty I suppose. As a doctor I'm used to dealing with bodily fluids, specimens. At medical school we were taught how to test for sugar in the urine in the case of diabetes, protein in the urine in kidney disease and so on; also blood in the urine with suspected cancer on the kidney or bladder cancer. Oh, you can tell a lot from the urine if you know what to look for.

He pointed at the rack of test tubes.

That's the key, of course: knowing what to look for. To the naked eye, that urine, most urine, looks completely innocent, even beautiful. Some people even drink urine! But don't be deceived, it's a poisoned chalice.

'Who is Alice and who poisoned her?' came a voice from the fluorophobe section of the audience.

Mousetit was not put off his stroke.

'Thank you, you might well ask. I'm looking for something in the urine that most doctors don't even suspect is there, let alone test for it. But I'm doing my own version of a test which is for a specific poison that I am certain is the cause of a great deal of ill health unbeknownst to many of the population including so called medical experts. I do my own test, devised it off my own back really from scratch from the textbooks because the sort of tests we learned at medical school, on the wards, in the surgery, are out of their league even if they were looking for it which they aren't'.

This was greeted by more barracking from the same section of the crowd: 'Shame', 'Typical', 'Dereliction of duty'…..

'I suppose I became aware of the problem four or five years ago. I kept seeing, as general practitioners do, a lot of people with vague complaints, feeling under the weather, not getting better with conventional treatments'…

This elicited cries of derision from the same hecklers: 'Lead swingers', 'Scroungers', 'They need to pull their socks up'….

Mousetit didn't let those go without an answer.

No, they were genuine sufferers. And then one day it sort of clicked into place.

'Arthritis, most likely, fluoride is known to cause clicking ' bellowed one of his supporters.

The chairman finally intervened: 'Please ladies and gentlemen, let Dr Mousetit finish his urine talk, don't spoil his flow'. Mousetit continued.

Thank you Mr. Chairman. As I was saying, I saw the light, the scales fell from my eyes. I was reading an article by an American medico, a doctor Struckoff, quite an eminent scientist really, that's what I reckon he was although he had been ostracized by many of his professional colleagues. Bit of a Lone Wolf really like myself suppose, he's been howling in the night about this issue for years, positively barking that's what he has been. I've been barking at the same thing. Anyway there it was, as clear as day. The answer to the prayers of all those sufferers and many more besides. It was all down to fluoride you see.

The fluorphobic section of the audience erupted on cue with, 'Shame', 'poison', 'filthy muck' and other odd expletives.

Fluoride. Supposed to be good for the teeth. And some years ago they started adding to water....

More heckles: 'pollution, that's what it is'…, 'mass medication'….

And claimed that it not only prevented dental decay but that it was perfectly safe and so they were pushing for more and more fluoride in the water.

Little flecks of foam appeared at the corners of his mouth. As he spat out the words, splashes of spittle landed on the chairwoman's head. She pretended to ignore them.

And then I started doing some research of my own and in the local medical school library. Obscure papers here and there, needed searching out, yes, and putting together and adding up and seeing the wood for the trees so to speak, this was a common denominator, fluoride. It was a revelation.

This was greeted by a series of evangelical cries from you-know-who: 'Halleluiah', 'Mine eyes have seen the glory', 'Pass the tambourines Mabel' and others in a similar vein. I even saw one anti-fluoridation protester start to get out a football rattle but she was restrained by a colleague.

Now Mousetit had his gander up and his followers in the audience were up with him.

And then I started looking more closely and sure enough if you look up fluoride you find that it is linked with all sorts of conditions, arthritis, cancer and you name it, it's there. So I invented this test and started testing the urine of the patients in my practice. And found excess fluoride in the urine, a sure sign that they were ingesting too much of the stuff.

His hand swept towards the test tube rack brushing one a glancing blow. A little splash of urine sailed through the air and caught the chairwoman in the eye. She wiped it away as if it were a tear of sorrow.

Of course this momentous discovery was met with skepticism in so-called conventional circles. I tried to get news of my discovery published in medical journals. That's the way these things are legitimized. And of course the main-stream medical journals rejected the articles. I'm not a member of their club you see. The health mafia club. Its town and country that mob. Us yokels from the country don't count. I'm a country member.

Suddenly Epididymis sprang to life saying, 'Yes, I remember'.

I was rejected! Sure they said it was on the grounds of statistical errors, or that my research was flawed; all a smokescreen of course. A shameful whitewash!

He was now punching out the words with gusto. He went a bit far with the effort; some of his more emotive words were accompanied by a little fart. Professor Epididymis moved his chair away from Mousetit but the chairwoman pretended not to notice.

They're trying to stop me in my tracks, trying to sweep it under the carpet and of course the thought occurs to any sensible person that if this is going on people in high places are trying to bury something. More like trying to bury their mistaken belief in fluoride along with the dead bodies it causes.

The medical profession and dentists, who do they think they are? Putting this poison in the water. Hanging is too good for them.

The crowd were with him and they cheered when a voice shouted 'The fluoride mob ought to be well hung'.

All right, if it was to cure cancer, perhaps. But tooth decay, a disease brought on by modern civilization? The people who get dental decay need to stop eating bad food, being dirty and not bothering to brush their teeth or just go to dentist.

Anyway, I think it's serious enough to want to pursue this so I set up a company and we advertise and solicit patients to send us samples of the urine with a list of any symptoms or malaise that they made suffer from. I test the urine and nine out of ten of course it's down to the fluoride and I let them know how to avoid fluoride.

As I said on national television to the poisoners of our water "Desist"!

This he roared at the top of his voice. He immediately looked a bit sheepish and said to the chairwoman in a stage whisper,

I disgraced myself.

'In what way Dr Mousetit?' she asked sympathetically.

I'm afraid I filled my pants shouting out.

'What, on national television?'

No, just then when I repeated the expletive.

The chairwoman discretely moved her chair back and sat with our professor. Mousetit carried on regardless.

In the end I became very busy and I had to give up my general medical practice. Of course I didn't leave until I got my pension. So now I'm a free agent and I can concentrate on my crusade on fluoride. I come here to debate the issue with you. And I'm a master debater.

'You said it mate' piped up Epididymis with what I thought was a touch of mockery in his voice. He also had a satisfied look in his eye like I had not seen before.

So here I sit and say 'sod the establishment' although of course I'm part of the establishment; now I'm one of the experts.

So cheers'.

And without batting an eyelid he raised a phial of the urine and took a big gulp. The audience gasped then cheered. He really was taking the piss.

Mousetit was mobbed on the platform by supporters while the rest of the audience filed out of the Theatre completely bewildered by what they had seen. Some of us were skeptical that the fluorophobes could ever be a significant force, others were not so sure. I never forgot my first sighting of them in full flight.

12

They don't often take many teeth out under general anaesthesia these days but I witnessed it and some of its problems when I was a senior student. Even though we weren't allowed to actually do it as a student, we had to see teeth being extracted under general anaesthesia. This took place in The Gas room in the dental school. The Gas room was a large clinical area in the oral surgery department. It was four times the size of a standard dental surgery. There was a lot to get in.

In the middle of the Gas room was a large cast iron seat a bit like a barber's chair. It had been in the Birmingham dental school for many years. It was installed for the first time at the turn of the century two buildings ago. It had been transplanted when new schools were built to replace obsolete ones. The Gas room chair never became obsolete. There was nothing remotely like it.

It took four burly porters to shift it and even then they had to do it in small increments and all wear trusses to prevent hernias. The floor had to be specially strengthened to bear the weight. It was a beast of a thing but it needed to be. Patients to be put to sleep were strapped in and anaesthetised. The chair had to be robust enough to support the slumbering patient and the anaesthetist leaning over the back giving the anaesthetic. It also had to resist the often frantic tugging and pushing that was needed to remove teeth quickly while the patient was unconscious and insensitive to the pain. Everything else in the room was subservient to the chair.

Behind and to one side was the Gas machine. This looked like an early Soviet space rocket. It had cylinders strapped to its side, pipes leading here and there and dials, switches and levers wherever there was space. The whole contraption was on castors attached to its spindly legs. Dangling down the side of the machine were a series of long round cylinders. These contained the anaesthetic gases. They were colour coded so the machine was garlanded with blue and white paint making it look even more Heath Robinson.

There was a large pressure-cooker like contraption on the top. This was the bit of the machine that supplied the potent anaesthetic that really put people to sleep. The gases from the cylinders were too weak to work on their own. They were used to carry in the volatile agent that put patients out and to supply life-preserving oxygen. Between the Gas machine and the chair was space for the anaesthetist.

If the Gas room was idle there was little else to see except this central island of equipment. When it was in use, the large empty space was filled with portable paraphernalia and people. The walls were lined with many glass-fronted cabinets. In these were the tools of the oral surgery trade: forceps, chisels for bone, drills, levers, gougers, saws. There also were dressings, medicaments, gowns, towels and packing materials. In one cupboard were more complex medical instruments like blood pressure measuring machines and electric cautery equipment (human flesh could be sealed and made blood-free using an electric current - you definitely wanted to be asleep for that).

Other deeper cupboards contained trolleys and stools that were wheeled out as necessary. For example, the instruments for a surgical procedure would be laid out on a trolley out of sight of the patient and trundled into view when all those that were supposed to be asleep were.

It took a remarkable number of people to run a Gas session. Apart from the patient there were his or her immediate attendants: the dentist, the anaesthetist and the nurse. There were other people outside this intimate circle. Some were nurses who were runners, fetching and carrying instruments, specimen pots, dentures to be fitted, discarded teeth and bone. On many occasions there were also students, some dental, some nursing and trainee anaesthetists. But surprisingly all these people, many of whom weren't regulars, didn't get under each other's feet.

There was a graceful choreography to a gas room session. The whole process was like a barn dance. Everyone would loiter nonchalantly around the periphery of the room like wall flowers at a dance while the patient was escorted in, strapped to the chair and put to sleep. But once the patient was unconscious people would move back and forwards, to and fro without ever colliding and without any conversation other than the occasional comment from the lead clinicians. It was poetry in motion done to an inaudible refrain. Usually it all went without a hitch. I was there when it all fell apart.

When things go wrong in any sphere it is not usually because of one single component. Most disasters are multifactorial, a mixture of mechanical, organisational and human factors. What happened that day is no exception. It wasn't anyone's fault. It was an accumulation of mishaps.

Putting someone to sleep for an operation is a complex thing. Anaesthetists make a career of getting it right. We all hope they do. But things can go wrong.

They say it takes two to tango and the same applies to a successful general anaesthetic: there are two players, the anaesthetist and the patient. Either one can mess it up. If the patient is ailing it can make the anaesthetic complex. If the patient is fat or fit they might need more anaesthetic to put them to sleep than their unfitter or slimmer equivalent. Likewise an inexperienced or incompetent anaesthetist might turn a simple gassing into a disaster. Both applied on that occasion.

There were both patient and anaesthetist factors at play that day. The anaesthetist was an inexperienced trainee. It happened a lot in those days. Dental general anaesthetics were regarded either as a nuisance or *a piece of cake* or sometimes both. The dental school anaesthetists were supplied by the neighbouring general hospital. Anaesthetists regarded the dental school a demotion if they were sent there rather than give the gas for a heart operation or on the labour ward. Sometimes we in the dental school got the runt of the anaesthetic litter. That day was one of those.

Even if we got an experienced anaesthetist we didn't always get the cream of the crop. Panic Annie was one such. Her real name was Dr Anne Tinkle but her tendency to panic during a case landed her with that nickname. For many years taking teeth out under general anaesthesia had been a job for the speedy. Before the invention of potent and safe chemicals to put people to sleep, the anaesthetists of old used many crude techniques, a popular one being the Anoxic Method.

This anoxic technique involved forcing a patient to breathe pure nitrous oxide until they turned blue (a sign that they had been rendered unconscious through a lack of oxygen) then allowing them to breathe air and slowly recover, meanwhile expecting the dentist to do his business before it was too late and the patient came round. It induced a sense of panic in both the dentist and the anaesthetist. Dr Tinkle took it more to heart than most.

When modern anaesthetics arrived she lost the need to panic and became a busybody. Freed from the tyranny of reviving the patient from deep anoxia, she would wander about the surgery pontificating on other people's work. It used to get up the noses of the dentist, the scrub nurse, even the occasional pathologist in attendance to look at specimens of flesh hacked out during a surgical procedure. The junior staff decided to teach her a lesson.

Dr Tinkle was also a self-appointed expert on car maintenance. She prided herself in doing everything to keep her car on the road thus gleefully depriving decent mechanics of her hard-earned money. Bored soon after the patient was asleep she would sniff round the surgery poking her nose into other people's work. While telling people how to do their jobs she would boast how much she had saved that week adjusting her carburettor, balancing her wheels or fitting a new turbocharger.

One day while she was engrossed in this business the houseman was sent to find her car in the staff car park. For a week he was instructed to siphon off half a gallon of petrol every day (those were the days before locking petrol caps). After one week, he changed tactic and added one gallon to the tank daily.

This continued for over a month. She soon noticed that her petrol consumption was fluctuating. She tried to normalise it but it refused to settle. The longer it went on the more desperate she became. Every gas room session became a must-attend occasion because of her despair and frustration. She ended up taking her engine to bits but it made no difference. Eventually she gave in and booked it in to a garage. The petrol tinkering was stopped. Her garage found nothing wrong, had just changed the plugs and her car reverted to normality. She was a broken woman and many pounds poorer.

We were spared Panic Annie that day but the anaesthetist we got wasn't up to snuff. That wouldn't have mattered if it weren't for the patient. The poor soul due to have a tooth out was thirty two stone Klondike Bill. He was a professional wrestler who won matches by dropping his huge body onto unsuspecting opponents as they lay momentarily stunned on the canvas. He was a big lad. And it wasn't all fat. He was also extremely fit. It took a lot of effort to haul his enormous body round the wrestling ring for ten rounds a bout. So he was fat and fit, and would need a lot more anaesthetic than most as any experienced anaesthetist would have known. But we had a real duffer.

When someone goes under a general anaesthetic the aim is to render them unconscious and insensitive to pain. It also helps if they have no memory of the event. That blissful state was called the surgical plane of anaesthesia. But you didn't go straight there if you were on the receiving end of an anaesthetic. If you were put to sleep slowly you would pass through higher planes. If it went too far you could go to a deeper plane close to death. It was important to get on the right plane. These days anaesthetists use injections of potent chemicals to whisk their patients to the surgical plane of anaesthesia quickly and uneventfully. At that time most patients were put to sleep by gas, a much slower method. So you might linger on your way to the surgical plane.

Just lighter than the surgical plane of anaesthesia is the plane of excitement. It is aptly named. Dwell here and you appear to be soundly asleep. Indeed if the surgeon sticks anything into you, you would not remember a thing. But you would react. Patients in this plane respond to any painful stimulus, sometimes violently. They will remain asleep but can do a form of sleep-walking involving all sorts of unpredictable things like lashing out. Little did we appreciate that we were heading in that very direction.

I didn't know any of this as I waited at the side of the room while the surgery was set up ready for the extraction. But there was one more complication. To cap it all there was a photographer present. He was from the University and he was taking pictures for the official calendar, and he'd come to take a photograph of somebody having their teeth out under gas. He wasn't happy because he'd turned up on the bus with all his equipment and it had taken him two hours to get there. He was told to wait with us bystanders until the patient had been settled when the dentist would indicate that he could come forward and snap a few pictures. The scene was set.

The door opened and Klondike Bill was escorted to the chair. We all looked away and pretended to mind our own business. The anaesthetist strapped Klondike Bill into the chair. He was a very big man. The lap strap strained to hold him down in the seat. The anaesthetist leaned over him, put the rubber anaesthetic mask over his nose and mouth and began to induce anaesthesia. He seemed to take a long time to settle.

Eventually the anaesthetist said 'Yes, you can go ahead now.'

'Are you sure' asked the dentist who was not quite as green at the business as his gassing colleague.

The anaesthetist said confidently: 'Oh he's well gone. Off you go'.

The complicated dance routine started. The scrub nurse pulled over the trolley and positioned it in front and to one side of the slumbering patient. Another nurse pulled out a stainless steel bowl and positioned herself by one of the patient's ears ready for any blood and debris. The dentist stood in front of the patient with a pair of forceps in his hand. Yet another nurse came forward with a gag to force open the jaws of the sleeping wrestler. The dentist gave one last nod at the anaesthetist and put the forceps blades on the offending tooth. And pushed down.

Most people know the phrase 'blood-curdling scream' but not many have heard a good one. Certainly they have not heard one as curdling nor as loud as the one that day. It was that bad it rattled windows. Imagine a fog horn up close but ten times worse because he was a big man with huge powerful lungs.

'Arghhhh' he went.

We spectators pressed hard against the walls.

The scrub nurse backed away. She guessed what was coming.

'Arghhh' he went on.

The anaesthetist gripped the mask tighter over the patient's nose.

Then the patient got up, all thirty two stone of him with the chair strapped to his buttocks. The anaesthetist rose up with Bill's back clinging on to his head trying to keep the gasses flowing into his nose. Then the wrestler raised his arms and grabbed the dentist by the throat. The dentist staggered backwards. The wrestler staggered forward keeping his grip tight around the extractor's throat and carrying the chair and the anaesthetist with him. It was a bizarre procession. The anaesthetist, two feet off the ground and looking like a teenage Ninja Turtle, scrabbled frantically to increase the flow of the sleeping mixture.

Eventually the convoy faltered. As the patient succumbed to the gasses so he slumped down and sat back in the chair. The anaesthetist welcomed his soft landing and we spectators all breathed a sigh of relief. The dentist lost his purple hue, recovered his composure, grabbed the forceps and reapplied them. All was calm. He looked toward the photographer but he had gone. The dentist shrugged and took out the tooth and the episode ended as had been planned with Bill awake and groggy but spitting blood into the proffered dish. He was quite used to this from his wrestling days so he seemed quite at home.

What of the photographer? Apparently when there'd been the blood-curdling scream he had gone pale, there had been a nasty smell in the surgery and he'd left the room. He was last seen waddling out of the anaesthetic department with all his equipment.

What a terrible waste of the photographer's time. Two hours there, two hours back, filled his pants and never even got his lens cap off.

13

Your time at dental school goes too quickly. There is a lot to get in so you don't see the speed at which you are learning and the huge amount of skill and experience you are acquiring. Between Optech one and Optech two we rotated though a number of departments in the school learning about false teeth in prosthetics, gums in the periodontics, x-rays in radiology, diagnostics in the examinations unit and what's now called public health in community dentistry.

Later on we would spend more time in the more influential departments, that is those areas of dentistry we might have to practice as soon as we graduated: oral surgery (taking teeth out and related topics), children's dentistry (including teeth straightening in orthodontics) and denture making (a longer spell in prosthetics). We would also see medical and surgical conditions that it was essential to be familiar with so we could not kill or injure a sick patient through ignorance of their general health.

We broadened our dental education by seeing things on the periphery like pathology (including autopsies), forensic medicine, drug and therapeutics and general anaesthesia. We knocked off rites of passage steadily: the first tooth extraction, the first child patient, the first general anaesthesia (in those days dentists were taught how to give them), the first post-mortem. Eventually we were ready to meet the outside world as newly-qualified dentists.

Before all that I had to pass finals. How I did I will never know. The written exams were as usual, a hard slog but we were used to that. It was the practical we sweated over. The final practical exam was the culmination of our dental undergraduate education. It was aimed at assessing the most common procedure we would be called on to do in the outside world – restore a decayed tooth. To test that skill we would all have to find a patient that needed a simple filling and make sure they turned up on the day of the examination. That was a feat on its own.

All our regular patients were treated to exhaustion. Every last nook and cranny had been renovated, every crown cemented, dentures settled and in constant use and gums clean, dapper and healthy. Our patients had become well trained. They could floss and brush until their enamel sparkled. They were as clean as a whistle and their whistles were clean. If you hunted for bacterial plaque (the cause of much dental disease) you couldn't find a fleck even if you used the usual method of staining it with disclosing solution. There was none to be disclosed. No, there was no point presenting one of our regulars for finals. There was nothing to be done. You had to get a stranger.

There were stacks of new patients at the dental school; they were often seen literally queuing at the front door. In those days, dental treatment was in short supply so even though it was done by students, the free dentistry at the dental school was just the job if you had a mouth full of dental caries and lots of time on your hands. Unfortunately new patients were not schooled: they didn't know what was expected of them (sit still, turn up regularly and lose track of time) they were unreliable and they might not get there on the appointed finals day. It was a gamble but we had to take the risk. So come the day it was tense all round.

We all had the jitters but couldn't show it. Everything we did was scrutinised by pairs of examiners, one from our own staff and one visiting.

The external examiners were the ones that mattered. It was assumed that the home team would be lenient on us poor examinees, not only because they had taught us all we knew, and a fail would reflect badly on them; but also because any of us who failed this final hurdle would have to resit the exam, so we would be a continued burden to them just as they were getting shot of us. The years behind us were pressing hard (for space, tutor time, for patients) so the staff wanted us to qualify come what may. Hence the externals were there to make sure we merited a pass and that the unsuspecting public were reasonably safe from our faltering first efforts.

As the exam progressed it was looking less and less likely that I would pass. I had exasperated the examiners. I was doing reasonably on the tooth I was supposed to be restoring. I had given a successful local anaesthetic. I had drilled an almost perfect cavity. I had not exposed the nerve in the tooth, a rare but game-changing mishap that meant the tooth had to be root filled which would add at least two more visits for the patient. No, so far so good.

But the examiners were not satisfied. They kept returning to look at the cavity but would not let me move on, to line it before filling. There was something I had missed but I couldn't see it – and the examiners weren't able to help me out because of the strict rules of conduct.

The more I looked, the less I saw, the more I panicked. In desperation I moved to the other side of the patient and peered in, this time getting a view I had not had before. This was my last chance. If I couldn't see what was bothering the examiners I would have to break out of the examination protocol and let them take over the management of the patient. Then I saw it. It was the tooth next door that was the problem. It had a hole in it I had uncovered drilling out the neighbouring tooth. As soon as I saw it I made the necessary comments to the examiners, they sighed their relief and I was back on track. Just a bit more drilling to deal with the new cavity.

I had sensed that I was on squandered goodwill as I ploughed on so when it happened I was completely flummoxed. Our slow drills were driven by a belt and pulley arrangement. This mechanical setup was crude but effective. The torque you could generate in your drill bit was impressive though dangerous to the health of the tender parts of the mouth. But we knew no better as we drilled ruthlessly, the smell of burning tooth substance giving away how close we were to scorching the fleshy pulp of the tooth. Patients would often stare mesmerised by the belt whizzing round the pulleys just inches from their head, marvelling at how close to danger we all were and how it all passed so uneventfully. Until that day during my finals patient.

Suddenly there was this almighty ripping sound followed immediately by my face getting swiped so hard I fell back off my stool. While trying to get up I heard a rhythmic slap-slap just like a blown car tyre hitting the rim as it slowed down the speeding car after a puncture. I looked up gingerly not sure what I would see. I didn't understand what it was at first.

There was some sort of hairy animal running up and down the arms of the dental engine belt drive. It was sticking closely to the belt like it was attached. It reminded me of the hare at a greyhound race that runs on a high-speed wire in front of the competitor dogs to encourage them to go fast. Like the hare, this hairy apparition was travelling at a frenetic pace. Then I realised what it was.

The hairy bundle of fur sprinting round the belt drive was actually my patient's toupee. I realised he was wearing one early on but feigned ignorance. I tried not to pull it off as I leant round his head to minister to his mouth. But the belt drive hadn't been so obliging. It had whipped it off. My patient was sitting there rubbing the previously-glued areas of his scalp looking sheepish and put out.

Then the toupee shot off the belt and skidded across the floor. The nearest external examiner jumped on it and stamped it furiously thinking it was some sort of vermin that needed annihilating.

There was panic among the nursing staff and a few patients ran for the waiting area with all sorts of dental ironmongery hanging out of their mouths. One novice nurse turned green, screamed and was last seen running out of the front door, never to be glimpsed again. Her friends told us she was convinced the animal laboratory on the top floor was breeding very aggressive, giant earwigs and that one had escaped and tried to attack her. I was convinced I had caused all this and that I was for the high jump.

I finished my examination case in a trance. I assumed my chances of passing finals were now completely shot. I was wrong. Apparently I was so distracted by it all I did the whole treatment session on auto-pilot. I lined the cavity with zinc oxide beautifully; I applied a perfect metal matrix band to prop up the fourth wall of the cavity while I mixed and condensed amalgam into the hole; I finished the job with a prefect carving, removed the matrix band, adjusted the occlusion, took out all the cotton wool rolls and bid the patient a fond expectoration. He left fully restored and the examiners passed me. I have never done a filling quite as well since then.

14

The thrill of passing finals was short-lived. It lasted a few days until we realised we had to find work. In those days we were spoilt for choice: there were no shortage of jobs, all you had to do was to decide what branch of dentistry you wanted to go into then very soon after you could get an interview and start almost immediately.

It was a far cry from today when jobs are scarce and competition stiff. Of course we didn't realise how lucky we were. We still whinged but it was about too much choice not too little. And to someone like me who had drifted so far it was an open invitation to drift some more.

I went through a series of posts when I left dental school. First I worked in the school dental service. That was a salaried job working for the local authority (a local government organisation that managed infrastructure and services for the population of a town).

Not satisfied with that (and frankly bored a lot of the time), I drifted into general dental practice. That was busier, had more variety and paid better even though it was piece work (fee-per-item-of-service). The nurses were prettier but the hours were longer. And it was insular; soon after I started there it dawned on me that if I stayed in this or any other general practice I faced working in the same surgery with the same set of people for many years, even the rest of my professional life. I wasn't ready for that yet. So I looked to get back into the hospital life where I imagined the action to be.

I began work as a senior house officer in the dental hospital. This was the service side of the dental school. It was in the same building but was organisationally separate from the school. It concentrated on treating patients with some postgraduate training for junior staff like me. I was at the bottom of the pecking order. Above me were the training grades of registrar and senior registrar. The consultant grade was the principal substantive post in the hospital.

There were other established dentists: academic staff were university employees but had equivalent grades to the service side; and there were salaried dental officers who were not consultants but did a lot of the day-to-day dentistry that didn't need highly specialised knowledge or experience. As you would imagine, this mixture was potentially explosive.

Beneath the surface the dental hospital and school was a mass of petty rivalry, intrigue and backstabbing. The service side hated the university side. The University employees (professors, senior and junior lecturers with a few research associates and assistants) assumed the service side was slow-witted and ignorant.

The Service staff regarded the academics as lazy and aloof. Added to this atmosphere was the usual junior-senior gulf: junior staff regarded their seniors as out of touch, old-fashioned and controlling; seniors resented the junior staff because they thought they were cheeky upstarts who were unworldly and woefully ignorant.

Then there was the salaried versus career conflict: the officers (who did most of the hum-drum work) resented the consultants and their juniors and the academics because they thought they were superior; and the salaried staff were looked down on by everyone else because they were sub-consultants and therefore lower caste.

To cap it all, the dentists had to rub shoulders with the nurses (a hierarchical mob if ever there was one) and the other workers in the building (porters, engineers, mechanics, laboratory staff, secretaries and so on). Students and patients were ignorant of it but the place was teeming with pent-up negative emotion. And I wanted to be part of it.

The bit that interested me most was the more medical side, anything to do with disease that wasn't just dental. I was intrigued by more than teeth. I wangled some work on the wards with inpatients. Oral surgeons were the ones that were more medical so I latched on to them. I found myself regularly in oral surgery outpatients. I loved to hear the tales my colleagues told.

The clinician who took me under his wing was the oral surgery registrar in the adjacent general hospital. There he and his boss got on quietly looking after head and neck trauma, cancer and other conditions that needed knowledge of the teeth but which also involved work in the surrounding structures even in other parts of the body.

An oral surgeon might mend a broken jaw with a bone graft but he would harvest the bone from the donor site on the hip bone. You had to know more than dentistry to be an oral surgeon and that attracted me.

My registrar seduced me with tales from the oral surgery clinic. He said oral surgery had been the passport to another world, the world beyond teeth. He had once been syringing out an antral sinus and that got him a night out with a patient. I wanted that sort of passport.

The maxillary antrum is a space in the upper jaw bone. Developmental and evolutionary biologists tell us the spaces like the antrum allow the bony skull to be lighter than if the bone was all solid. They insist we can hold our heads high because of the ingenious honeycombed architecture.

Whether that is true or not the antrum can become infected and that's where the oral surgeon comes in – he doesn't step literally into the antrum but he has to wash it out. It becomes infected because it is connected to the nose and after a head-cold (known as coryza) infective organisms can travel into the antrum and multiply.

The symptoms of sinusitis are known to most people for this common ailment causes pain and discomfort above the eyes and around the face as fluid from the infection pools. The oral surgeon can relieve the pressure by doing an antral washout.

Being dentists at heart, the oral surgeon prefers to go into the antrum from the mouth. A wide-bore needle is thrust up the outer gum and into the offending space just above the upper teeth. Sterile fluid can then be injected to wash away the sepsis which drains back down the nose from where it came in the first place. It sounds gruesome but it is very effective. But it doesn't always turn out as expected.

The patient was a very attractive young woman so my registrar was showing off, making every move with a flourish and giving a smooth and calming commentary as he went about the business.

'I'll just inject a little anaesthetic to numb the gum before I start' said he.

'Thank you very much' said she.

'Now you'll feel a little pressure as I slide in the needle' he continued.

'Be gentle with me doctor' she whispered as she fluttered her eyes.

'There, you didn't feel a thing, did you?' was his silver-tongued reply.

'You are kind' she murmured as he carried on.

He pushed the syringe plunger and injected the washout under firm but constant pressure as he purred 'There, nearly over'.

'Woops' she exclaimed as her eye shot out.

'Blimey!' was all he could manage as he saved the eye from falling on the floor.

Then it was her turn to wipe his sweaty brow. She explained that she had lost her eye in a childhood accident and the one he had just popped out was only glass. Relieved, he recovered his composure and embarked on a long and complicated explanation of what had just happened, rapidly remembering the mechanics of the embarrassing incident.

'I know what happened. The antrum is just below the eye socket and sometimes there is a small hole connecting the two. My high pressure washout obviously escaped into the orbit and pushed out your eye.' He sat down to recover his composure and added a paltry 'sorry' to round off his explanation.

The patient was more laid-back than my registrar. She told him not to worry, that there was no harm done, it could have happened to anyone, and why didn't she cheer him up by taking him out after the clinic. He limply agreed because he felt so mortified. It was much later when they were in the pub and he was smoking a cigar and nursing a brandy did he recover some of his bravado. Now they were both mellow he hazarded a question.

'I hope you don't mind me asking but do you always treat your medical attendants as royally as this'?

She put her drink down and came right out with it. 'No, you're.....'

He was expecting some appropriate compliment like 'You're so dashing', or 'What a handsome guy you are' or even 'you're my hero'.

But all she said was: 'No, you're the first doctor that's caught my eye'.

It was tales like that that made me hanker after doing medicine. You'd think I would have been happy enough to qualify and get away from the undergraduate world soon after graduation and I was for a while. But the more time I spent in oral surgery and the more contact I had with the world of medicine the more I wanted to do it. And the budding oral surgeon had the perfect excuse to go back to medical school: you had to have a medical degree if you wanted to be a top oral surgeon. But I had always fancied doing medicine anyway, oral surgery or not.

15

Doing medicine as a second degree was rare in my day. Career pathways were more rigid, people didn't change course so often and if you made the wrong choice to start with you made the best of a bad job. But that was changing. The world of my immediate predecessors was a rigid one: you took exams and the result sealed your fate. By the time I came through the education system the faults were beginning to be rectified.

Even so, it was a difficult decision to go on to do medicine after dentistry. I had to get in to medical school, find the finance to see me through and think hard about what I would do at the end of it all. Being a dental graduate didn't count for that much with the admissions people. If you got an interview you had to argue hard that you deserved a place over school leavers.

You had to play the oral surgery card carefully: if you swore you wanted to do medicine to go into oral surgery, some admissions panels thought you were just using the medical degree as a ticket to a non-medical career and that you were, in effect, wasting the place. On the other hand if you defused the oral surgery issue other members of a panel might play the age card and refuse admission because you would be too old to make a career of your doctor's degree.

As was typical of me I tried to play both cards at once, not being able to make my mind up so going for the compromise. As it happened it worked but I felt no shame. I really did want to do medicine and it wasn't just to get on in oral surgery.

I was originally inspired to go into medicine because of my father. He was a general medical practitioner. His stories of interesting cases made me want to join his club.

He was closing up his surgery one night and a man appeared at the door.

He said, 'Doc, I know you're shutting up shop but could you take some stitches out? I've been to the hospital and had some put in my ear but I don't want to go back there to have them taken out. It's a long way to go just to have stitches removed and I don't like hospitals anyway. Can't you do them here? '

Reluctantly he said, 'Come on in'.

He took the stitches out of his ear and the man said, 'And I've got some stitches down below as well. Would you mind taking those out?' And sure enough, he had some stitches in his wedding tackle.

My father said, 'Well, tell me what on earth happened? '

The man told his story. 'I was walking home from the pub one night and I needed to pass water. I had a full bladder after all the beer I had drunk and I was desperate. So I went down this alleyway. After I had relieved myself I was a bit too hasty pulling up the zip of my trousers. I got the skin of my scrotum caught in my zip. It was agony and I couldn't free it.

My friends carried me home and they laid me on the floor in the kitchen and they said, 'We'll give it a yank, and it will be painful but, you know, we'll free everything up.' And they did that and I screamed so much my dog came over and bit me on the ear.'

Of course the world of medicine wasn't all funny or heart-warming anecdotes and for years I pushed all thoughts of being a doctor to the back of my mind while I studied dentistry. But even during our dental training I would come into contact with the world beyond teeth and it would stir up all the old feelings again. Like the time I was assigned to shadow an ambulance driver.

Even all those years ago, our dental course was a bit progressive. We were given the odd look into the world outside dentistry. For example we were taken down a working deep coal mine. It affected us dental students in different ways. Some envied the honest toil of the working man, some looked romantically at the comradeship, others liked the hard physical toil compared our sedentary occupation peering into the human mouth day in and day out. My overwhelming feeling was one of relief – relief that I didn't have to work in those conditions of heat and dirt, that my job was white-collar, that I was a professional and had a respected status in the community.

I was glad to experience the coal face but was heartily relieved to get back into my cosy little environment. But spending some time with an ambulance driver sounded like a lot of fun, what with the gory sights I was sure to see and being driven to them in a big vehicle with flashing lights and a siren was a boy's idea of bliss. I was already a fan of the big vehicle. While I was a student I had qualified as a bus driver, taking my Public Service Vehicle license lessons on a Sunday morning driving a huge double decker bus.

I spent a fortnight with the ambulance driver. In those days it was just me, the student, and the ambulance driver journeying around answering calls. Nowadays there is a team in each vehicle, including paramedics and sometimes a doctor. Then it was a one man affair.

While we were out one day a call came through on the intercom that there was a riot in the town centre and that there'd been a casualty right in the middle of the area. This sounded exciting to me and not a little dangerous. I sat up in the passenger seat in a state of anticipation and tightened my seat belt.

We drove up to the riot area of the town, but the ambulance driver didn't stop at the edge of the rioting, he just drove straight on through the crowd. They were banging on the side of the ambulance, rocking it back and forward and shouting obscenities at us. It was frightening. I was terrified. He just kept driving on in.

We eventually got to the casualty. We stopped, opened the back doors of the ambulance, lifted the patient in and sped off to the hospital. Then went back to the ambulance base. The controller was there.

He said 'Well done lads that was marvellous. What an act of courage. You drove up to the edge of the rioting and most people would have stopped and waited for a police escort. But you drove straight on in to get your casualty. Have tomorrow off'.

He said to the ambulance driver, 'What are you going to do with your day off'?

The driver replied ruefully 'I'm going to take the ambulance and get the blasted brakes fixed'.

The excitement of it all just fuelled the idea I wanted to do medicine even more. But it was earthier than that. Looking back I realise now I was a bit inadequate. I had grown up a lot since I went to dental school but still lived in a relatively sheltered world. Yes I had mixed with arty types at the student union, even had intimate contact with a few of them. And I had been involved in extra-curricular activities more than most dental students who confined themselves to sport and drinking alcohol.

The world of dentistry was beginning to close in on me. I saw my colleagues narrow their perspectives: everything revolved around the mouth (their job, their professional circle, even some of their social life when they married fellow dentists) and everything was measured in dental terms. I began to hear my dental friends become obsessed with what they could earn in dental practice or the status and power they could achieve in the university or hospital domain. Colleagues even admired items of clothing in shops and measured their cost not in how much they would have to spend to acquire the item but how many crowns they would have to fit or teeth they would have to extract. It was all a bit pedestrian for me. I wasn't ready to settle, not for that sort of mundane existence.

It's part of the desperation business this wanting power and status and dentistry didn't deliver all I wanted. There is a pecking order in the health care world but it is not easy to work out the rules. I came face-to-face with this years later after I qualified in medicine and started what was then called General Professional Training.

After medics finished their apprenticeship year as house doctors and when they got their full registration with the General Medical Council, they did a series of six-month jobs in a mixture of specialties. We were senior house officers, the first rung in the service medical and surgical hierarchy. I did obstetrics and gynaecology, psychiatry, general medicine and community medicine. After this spell at SHO level most doctors would then proceed to a full-time hospital or general practice training grade. But while we were at this lowly level and swapping jobs on a regular basis, the pecking order issue came up and bit me on the bottom.

In my small dental world I was used to a pretty stable status. You are a dentist whatever job you do, whether in hospital, the community or general practice. Even academic dentists were dentists. Only oral surgeons got uppity about whether they were medics or dentists. Some didn't want to be tarred with the dental brush maintaining it kept them back; others were proud of their dental roots as it gave them a set of skills the medics never developed. But now I was in the Senior House Doctor business rank suddenly became much less certain.

My status would change with my job. One day I might be a psychiatrist, the next an obstetrician. I didn't know any more or less about the respective specialities, I was just part of a different tribe from one six month period to the next. But the world saw me differently. In my general medical post I was relatively high status. We handled serious diseases like heart attacks and strokes so we were in demand throughout the hospital.

When I was a psychiatrist I was immediately demoted status-wise. Now I was dealing with a different group of patients who were sometimes regarded by society as a race apart. I was rarely asked to see medically sick people so I occupied an obscure orbit away from the main stream.

When I then did obstetrics, suddenly I was in demand again, but only under certain circumstances. We were ignored most of the time, even ridiculed as obstetricians (after all, that was *women's affairs*). But if a pregnant woman turned up in the main hospital and she was in labour we were given the red carpet treatment until she was safely carted away. None of this cultural baloney made any sense and I suspect much has been ditched. But at the time it was a burdensome part of our world and none more so than the status issues between medicine and all other professions.

Our colleagues were regarded by the doctors (and others) as inferior. Dentists were no exception to this rule so it made an impressionable desperado like me want to remedy the problem. Any sensible adult would have worked on his self-esteem but no, I went the long way around. I was sure if I became a doctor it would make me a better person, more respected and with a higher status. I was seduced by the myth of the high-status medic as I thought it would make me high status too. I assumed the new-found elevated status would bring acclaim, riches, adoration and, most of all, power. What a fool.

Dentists had a bit of power but it wasn't enough for me. The dentist wields power over the patient as long as the patient is beholden to the dentist. It is an unhealthy relationship looked at like that but it is true. The good dentist doesn't exploit that power but tries to have a more positive relationship with the patient in their care. But some dentists exploit their position and it can be satisfying in a shallow sort of way. I had learnt about the fickle nature of this sort of power when I worked in general dental practice.

Dentists can sometimes brow-beat patients because they can literally stop them talking when they put all that paraphernalia in their mouths: saliva ejectors, suckers and the like. Then the sadists among them ask questions and you can't answer:

Dentist: 'How's the wife?'

Patient (mouth crammed with equipment): 'Gurgle, wssh, scorf, muggle'.

I used to enjoy this simple act of dominance but it came back to bite me. Or rather, the patient did.

One time I was treating a young woman. I put the saliva ejectors and the suckers in packed well with cotton wool rolls and sheets of muslin gauze. I made sure she couldn't speak before I grilled her about her holiday plans.

I said 'Where you going on holiday?'

She said 'I'm going to Italy.' At least that's what she intended to say and I fully understood it because I was very experienced at interpreting conversation filtered through a mouthful of metal and plastic. But to a bystander it would have sounded like 'Frime gaggling poo frittering'.

'Italy' I said, 'You won't like Italy, it's a horrible place.'

It's the whole power thing, you see. I was trying to humiliate her, make her feel small for having chosen to go to a place not approved by me.

I said 'What hotel?'

She spluttered her reply.

I looked scornfully at her up-turned eyes and sneered, 'Oh you won't like that hotel, it's a horrible hotel, very expensive and dirty, the staff are money grabbing. And I wouldn't go and see the Pope. No. St Peter's square, you won't actually see the Pope, it's terribly crowded.'

Ha, I thought I had completely humiliated her; instant gratification for me.

She came back from holiday determined to get her own back. I could tell by the look in her eyes that she would brook no interruption. She said to me 'Before you put that saliva sucker thing in, we had a wonderful time in Italy.'

'Oh', I said, rather put out.

She went on 'It was a marvellous hotel, cheap, clean and the staff were lovely.'

'Oh', I said, rather more peeved that she had turned the tables on me. But she just kept throwing it at me, giving me the same as I had given her, trying to humiliate me.

I rallied and said, 'I bet you didn't see the Pope.'

I had fallen for her trap, so she gleefully pounced, 'Oh yes we saw the Pope, of course we saw the Pope. We went to St Peter's square, in fact he got into the little pope-mobile, he came all the way across St Mark's square and he got out right in front of me. Do you know what he said to me?'

'No' I said.

With a broad smile on her face she landed the killer blow, 'The Pope said in a really loud voice 'who's ruined your teeth then?!'

I then realised if I wanted to get more power I would have to become a doctor. There was no turning back. Though I was foolish and naïve, I assumed being a doctor would remedy some of my deficiencies. Of course it didn't work out like that but I was desperate.

16

I tried to go to medical school in Birmingham but I couldn't get in so I went to Leicester. Birmingham was a long-established medical school but Leicester was new. The medical school there had only opened a year or so before I entered. It had been planned as a new type of medical school compared to the old style like Birmingham. You might think training a doctor is pretty orthodox, that graduates of all medical schools must be the same as each other but they aren't. Sure, the General Medical Council and the other governing bodies make sure there is a minimum standard and that doctors from any source can function in the prevailing state of the medical art. But within those strict boundaries there are variations.

The big difference I experienced was between the *old* medical curriculum and the *new*. Leicester had a newly-minted course so was free to introduce modern concepts in medical education. These included a shift from basic sciences (like anatomy) towards social sciences.

Our course had a lot more sociology, psychology and communication skills input than traditional schools. This recognised the shifting world of the doctor-patient relationship from a science-based blinkered approach to a more humanitarian view of the challenges faced in the battle with ill-health. So we were to major on people and their predicament rather than focus exclusively on disease and treatment. The approach recognised the limitations of scientific medicine and tried to bolster the humanitarian aspect.

I found the new curriculum much easier as an older (mature) student. There was less emphasis on rote learning and more on understanding. Pure science was diminished, softer social science was to the fore. As life skills were appreciated more this new recipe for being a doctor was easier for a mature student to cope with. I found it simpler to get on with family studies and dealing with sick people because I was older and more worldly-wise than my school-leaver colleagues. They outpaced me on the heavy subjects but I made up the differences in the softer areas. I passed all my exams and qualified as a doctor.

One of the first things I did when I knew I had passed medical finals was to go back to my old oral surgery world to see what my prospects were. I had kept an eye on the oral surgery business when I was a medical student always assuming that was where I was heading in the end. But the dream had begun to fade. I was mixing more and more with medics and I knew less and less about dentistry. From my new perspective the dental world seemed small and constricted. So I was interested to go back and see how the land lay for me and my future career pathway.

Returning to my old oral surgery domain was like going back to my childhood. Everything seemed so small: the surgeries, the diseases, the patients, the professionals. It was like I had been away from a small rural community to a big city only to return and find nothing had changed. Only I had seen the wider world. I immediately knew I wouldn't go back.

Anyway I was now a changed professional person since I had done medicine. From my early medical student days I realised the medical profession really was a different world from my previous dental existence. For example, I soon found out that medical students are more arrogant than dental students.

The first week we were having lectures we medical students used to go out into the quadrangle at lunchtime and try to recognise the patients coming into the hospital. You could hazard a guess at what was wrong by the demeanour: if they had strokes; or rashes; some of them had tremors, others discoloured skin or disfigured faces.

It was a lovely sunny day and my new fellow-medical student friend and I were sitting outside. We had only been to three lectures but we already thought we knew it all. A patient came walking up towards us. He had the most awkward way of walking, his hands in the air, his legs bowed and apart and he gingerly edged his way forward with a most disgusted look on his face. We were in diagnostic heaven.

My friend jumped straight in, he said 'I think, it's quite clear this man has got prolapsed piles.'

Being just as cocky as him, I said 'No, no. He's got an anal fissure. You know, he's split at the back.'

By this time the patient had come within earshot and he said 'No lads, we're all wrong. I thought it was a fart.'

I was off and running as a medic. This was the life for me, much more fun than dentistry and ruder as well. I was in my element. The rest of the training didn't disappoint. It was even better when we got to sexual medicine.

Like lay people, medical students have all sorts of fantasies about sexual medicine. But they soon have their eyes opened when they come into contact with patients. Like smokers and lung cancer, the glamorous side of a lifestyle choice soon pales when the hapless victim suffers the consequences. When I was a house doctor I worked on a respiratory ward. Part of my workload was to admit patients suffering from lung cancer. Most of them had been smokers. It was immensely sad to hear of their lives blighted by what they thought was one of their pleasures, smoking. There was no glamour in dying from a smoking-related disease. So it was with sexual medicine.

Most patients who need the services of sexual medicine have suffered at its hands. For all our bravado as medical students, and even though we thought we were thrill-seeking young people pushing the sexual barriers of the time, in reality we suffered very little harm.

Some patients had a rougher time physically or mentally from sexual relationships. We doctors had to learn about the casualties and how to patch them up. There was some sniggering at the fate of our patients but it was rare.

One day I was in what we would now call the department of genitourinary medicine but was then known as the Clap Clinic. The next patient was summoned and in came an elderly gentleman. Without any formalities he pulled open his fly buttons, got his todger our, slapped in on the desk and said 'Doc, I think it's caught a cold.' It's what's called a euphemism.

The clap doctor was a very wise man and a very honest doctor; I learnt a lot from him. He said 'Yes, it's caught a cold has it?' He lifted the offending organ up with his pencil and said, 'In that case, until it sneezes I'll treat it for syphilis'.

The rare amusing encounters continued as a medical student the next time we were in the same clinic. A young male patient came in complaining of a crop of warts on his penis. Most people encounter the odd wart or two on their hands but they can multiply and be a much bigger nuisance especially if there are a lot of them and they grow on the male organ. It puts off the sexual partners somewhat. And this lad had a whopper of a crop and he complained it was losing him girlfriends.

It had badly affected his sex life so he was desperate for treatment. In the past what used to be called venereal diseases were thought of as a punishment from God for sexual excess or misbehaviour. Therefore many of the treatments devised were designed to punish as well as cure. For example, an old cure for gonorrhoea involved inserting a miniature umbrella up the male urinary orifice and removing it after it had been opened up. It made even the toughest men cry and not just with remorse.

Modern treatments were not as cruel as those old-fashioned ones but in some of the old doctors there lurked a hankering for the good old days. Our boss that day was of that old school.

The doctor had just the treatment for the penile warts. It comprised a medicated type of sandpaper. The patient was instructed to take the sandpaper home and carefully use it to smooth away the warts from the penile surface. The patient sheepishly pocketed the packet he was given and told to report back in a week. We made sure we were there to see the results.

I thought the doctor was rather put out when the patient returned. When asked if he had used the sandpaper diligently and regularly he nodded yes. He fetched out what remained of it – it was worn all shiny and smooth. He was then asked how he was getting on with his girlfriends. The boy brightened up and replied, 'With that sandpaper who needs girlfriends?' The sandpaper was confiscated from him as the boss said he had 'overdosed' on it.

As much fun as these encounters in outpatients were, it was on the wards that we medics learnt to become real doctors. You soon discover that much of what goes on in medicine is not funny, to the patient anyway.

When I was a junior hospital doctor there was a very ill old lady dying on the ward. She was very posh, very refined. She had to be fed by a tube and all we could feed her was Complan, a thick bland nutritious milkshake that looks, feels and acts like wallpaper adhesive if it is mixed badly. She died one night and my registrar was with her. He said to me,

'Do you know what her final words were – her last words before she died? Just before she passed away, she whispered, 'No more effing Complan!''. But it wasn't just the patients that came out with the witty lines even if they were ironic. Sometimes it was the staff or even their relatives.

One day when I was coming out of the operating theatre changing rooms I came upon a woman who was having a go at one of the most attractive girls in our medical year. The woman was bright red in the face and she was hollering at the girl, 'You keep your eyes to yourself in that changing room, will you? My husband, he's the senior surgeon here and you've been putting it about that he's got a wart on his penis.'

The female student was made of stern stuff. She stood her ground saying, 'I didn't say that.'

The woman was a bit crest-fallen. She looked like she was about to take her words back when my student colleague ruined the effect by continuing, 'I never said your husband had got a wart on the end of his penis. I said it <u>felt like</u> he'd got a wart on his penis.'

The student's goose was well and truly cooked. She was soon transferred to another medical school and we never heard of her again. Pity because she missed some very interesting cases in our outpatient clinics.

When you start going into outpatients as a medical trainee you begin to learn a lot. One of the very first patients I saw was a miner – a coal miner – and he had a flat head and a cauliflower ear. As a good medical student I asked him the story of his condition and he was glad to tell me. He said, 'Well doc, I'm a hero. I was in the coal mine and there was a roof fall and I kept the roof up with my head and all my colleagues got out. So, I'm a hero but I ended up with a flat head.'

I wrote it all down then said, 'Well, that explains the flat head. What about the cauliflower ear?'

He said, 'That's where they hammered me in'.

Before long in your medical training you go on the wards where you spend a disproportionate time compared to the rest of your medical career. Most doctors work in general practice but medical students in my day did a lot of their training on hospital wards often treating very sick people. But not every patient in hospital is mortally sick. Most of them are but there's one group of people who aren't very ill and they can be found on the orthopaedic ward.

You often get a lot of young men who have broken their bones and they might lie in traction in bed for months on end as orthopaedic inpatients. They're not really ill, they are just waiting for the bone to heal. They get bored stiff and they're very frustrated. You can imagine that. And when I was a houseman on the ward they'd spend all their time in the physiotherapy, particularly off our ward. There was a very young female physiotherapist there.

One of my patients decided he wanted no more physiotherapy so I took the opportunity to ask him why this particular physio was so popular and why he was not seeing her anymore. My patient was candid and he let me in on the secret of our physiotherapist's popularity - she did relief massage (a medical term for manual manipulation of the genitalia, a euphemism for masturbation). That's why she was so much in demand. All the men were going in there every day for a bit of relief massage.

I said, 'Well, why did you stop?'

He said, 'Well, one day I was in there and she was doing the business, and I said to her, 'You handle my male anatomy very professionally.''

And she said, 'Well, I should do, because before the operation, I had one myself.' It put him right off.

Life as a doctor in training can seem chaotic but my world was settling down. I was now married and we had started a family. We were living in a small house in a pretty village outside Leicester. We put down roots and got into routines domestically and professionally. I continued to practice dentistry alongside medicine which meant we had extra income but the hours were long. I knew things couldn't go on like they were indefinitely and I would have to choose a long-term career but there were still professional avenues to explore. During my years of general professional training I got lots of experience of general medicine and surgery but I really hankered after doing something distinctive. So I headed for the maternity ward.

17

I had always wanted to do Obstetrics and Gynaecology after my first delivery as a medical student. I was so proud. I paraded round the labour ward showing off the new arrival I had delivered (with the help of a midwife). A visitor stopped and admired me and the baby. She said, 'Ooh, isn't he a lovely big boy?'

I was quick to reply, 'Two things madam: firstly it's a girl not a boy. And secondly that's my finger you're holding.'

Obstetrics and Gynaecology is one of those mystifying combinations. Lay people and green medical students don't understand why bits of the healing profession are carved up exactly as they are. Obstetrics in itself seems to most people enough of a job, looking after pregnant women and delivering their babies without worrying too much about the non-pregnant female.

You soon realise why this specialty has the boundaries it has. There is a continuum between the non-pregnant woman and her pregnant counterpart. Basically the specialty revolves around the womb and most things to do with it. But the O&G specialist cannot ignore the person around the womb, just as dentists can't just concern themselves with the mouth.

There is a lot of confusion at the boundaries between specialties and there fierce territorial battles may be fought. For example, if a woman has a problem with her breasts during pregnancy the general surgeon and the O&G doctors may fight over who is in charge. It makes for interesting clinical encounters and emphasises why doctors need to train in more than one specialty. But I was keen to mark out the O&G territory with a bit of my scent.

I got the chance as a junior O&G doctor and I jumped at it. Being a mature graduate helps a great deal in something like O&G. A lot of clinical medicine is about bluffing. My father qualified from Queen's University in Belfast and he was always proud they awarded their graduates a degree in the <u>Art</u> of Obstetrics and Gynaecology. Nowadays it is all evidence-based practice in the medical world and in my father's day I suppose there was a lot less evidence so there was more of an art to it.

As I progressed through my medical and dental career I came to believe that there was still a large element of art in the job, especially if you wanted to get on well with patients. I noted time and again that the most successful clinicians were artists first and not just piss-artists. So being more mature like I was helped pass me off as a more experienced doctor. It all facilitated getting by day to day while I built up experience.

There was a down side to being the mature student (later junior doctor). To fund my second degree I had to earn money so as a medical student I would moonlight as a dentist. I would work evenings and weekends as a dentist while during the day I was a medical student. It came back to bite me.

One day I was on the labour ward as a medical student sewing up a woman I'd just delivered. When women deliver a baby, it often pays to cut through the perineum and the side wall of the vagina to avoid tears from a large baby's head. This cutting is called an episiotomy and the flesh needs to be sewn back up if the woman is to resume normal sexual relations and not be incontinent or suffer a prolapse. The junior doctor gets the regular job of sewing up after an episiotomy. This was what I was doing that day, minding my own business – or rather, the business of the woman between whose legs I was sitting.

Suddenly her husband walked in and he only knew me as his dentist. The look on his face said everything; presumably he thought that I was his pervert dentist having cheap thrills on his wife. Just before he hit me I remember distinctly what he said: 'You won't find any teeth down there, you blaggard!'

By the time I was a proper doctor on the labour ward I had more experience of life than most and looked the part more convincingly. I was a lot older than my contemporary junior doctors who had qualified from the same medical year as me. But no matter how mature you think you are things can still surprise you. It happened one night when I did an internal examination on a mother nearing the second stage of labour when the baby is about to be born.

The internal vaginal examination is not enjoyed by either party. The woman on the receiving end would be unusual if she relished being manipulated by a relative stranger especially if she has been in labour for a long time and is tired, irritable and helpless on her back like a beached whale.

Likewise the doctor (or midwife) thrusting their hand into the pelvis of the woman is not particularly enjoying it either. It can be a stab in the dark so to speak. The clinician's hand has certain questions to answer: how dilated is the cervix of the womb, whether the baby is ready to be born, if there any obstructions to labour and so on.

Yet the answers don't necessarily come easily for it can be confusing in the labouring vagina if all you can use is your hand. No peeping is allowed unless you go a lot further and introduce instruments and a light; that is escalating the issue. No, you have to try to get the answers by feel only and it can be nerve-wracking. The examiner is often as tense as the woman. It's much, much worse if something grasps your hand when it's in the vagina.

Something grabbed hold of the tip of my finger as I was examining the woman that day. It gave me quite a shock so I withdrew my hand abruptly. At first the woman didn't react. She was dozing when I was examining her. After hours of labour she was too exhausted to complain about yet another invasion of her privacy and assault on her dignity. She just lay there and let me get on with it. But she must have sensed there was something wrong because when I snatched out my hand she opened one eye as if to say 'something wrong?' To allay her fears I just smiled and put my hand back in. I expected what had just happened was my mind playing tricks. It wasn't. There was that grabby thing again and this time it wouldn't let go.

I now know the explanation and it is relatively benign. Sometimes the emerging child is born with one arm over its head (most babies come out head first). The infant has a reflex in its hands – if the hand encounters anything it grabs hold. This is a charming phenomenon if the baby is being held in the arms of its loved ones and it evokes oohs and ahhs in bystanders. But I wasn't about to ooh or ahh; I was tempted to let out an oath because this stirred up a mythical fear some men have. And my mind leapt back to the encounter I had had under the circus seating. I half expected to hear a trumpeting as my hand was consumed.

Many men have a misplaced belief that some female internal genitalia have teeth - it is called Vagina Al Dente and it implies biting where biting would not normally be found. It is pure fantasy brought on by men's inferiority complex in sexual relations with women and I knew it was not true because I had seen the anatomy for myself. But the myth was a strong one and for a fleeting moment I had fresh doubts. I thought it had actually come true.

The woman reacted to my discomfort. She opened her bleary eyes wider and asked if the baby had been born yet.

'No' I said, 'But I nearly had kittens!'

The husband sat bolt upright, suddenly awake after his long snooze.

'Kittens? Ah, so that's why they call it a pussy'.

Fortunately I had an experienced and kind-hearted midwife with me. She realised what was happening and put me out of my misery. I was relieved it was an innocent phenomenon and the baby was delivered successfully shortly after. For a while though it made me sweat. Old men's tales can be just as potent as old wives'.

Away from the cut and thrust of the clinic and the labour ward professional life was still fascinating. When I was an obstetric junior doctor, we used to have regular clinical lecture-demonstrations. These were supposed to be educational but were usually taken by the consultant staff as an opportunity to humiliate junior staff. One time, though, they got their comeuppance.

The topic for the day was the overdue pregnancy. Our clinical case was a woman still undelivered at 43 weeks. She was lying calmly at the front of the lecture hall half asleep and not a sign of labour to be seen.

We were all watching the new doctor present the case and she was making use of the newly-installed computerised audio-visual equipment. At the appropriate moment she pushed the button to raise the projection screen and started to palpate the patients slumbering abdomen.

Unknown to us all, the bottom of the screen had caught on the patient's trolley and was under increasing tension as it tried to rise to the ceiling. Suddenly the tension was released. There was an enormous bang and the patient was thrown to the floor.

Amid the confusion, everyone forgot the patient until the junior doctor asked her how she was. 'I'm fine' she said 'but I need to push'. The snapping screen had done what £500 of drugs had failed to – induced labour.

'Where's my consultant' she gasped amid a fierce contraction.

'In the gents' replied the senior registrar. 'He couldn't resist the urge to push either but it ain't no baby'.

Nowadays I believe they use simulated patients and life-like dummies instead of real subjects. And at the time our hearts went out to the poor junior doctor that was making the presentation. We were still at that naïve stage in our careers when we hadn't developed the acute rivalry between professionals. But it was forming in our minds.

When I was an obstetric senior house officer I encountered hostility and malice from professional colleagues for the first time. Even as students we weren't aware how much hatred and back-stabbing there was on the wards and clinics, and the scalpels used for stabbing were often rusty as well. Junior medical and dental staff started to become rivals as they climbed the promotion ladder in their specialty. But that was nothing compared to the antagonism shown by some professional colleagues just because we were doctors.

This was especially acute on the Labour Ward. There were exceptions, but a good few midwives had it in for the junior doctors. It was partly that us medics were sitting ducks: even the most junior midwife knows far more about delivering babies than any newly-qualified doctor. But the hierarchy deemed that doctors were further up the medical pecking order.

This bred resentment in some midwifery co-workers and they would go out of their way to get us into trouble whenever they could. They would refer patients a bit too late so the clinical problem was a lot worse for the receiving doctor than it need have been. They would unload problem cases as soon as they could no matter how busy was the doctor. And they worked shifts so they could clock off and go home even if there was much more to do.

We used to have this horrible midwife. She was always trying to belittle us doctors, trying to make us look small, and as a junior doctor you're very vulnerable. She'd let you make mistakes, precipitate clangers for you to drop, embarrass you in front of patients and so on.

One day I came up onto the labour ward in the morning. In those days the midwives always used to line up beside the booking-in counter like taxi cabs on the rank. So when the woman came in in labour the first midwife would take her off, then the second would take the next and so on. That morning there was this great long line of midwives waiting, and at the end of the line was Sister Beans. She was the horrible sister. I spotted an opportunity to have my revenge.

I went up to the first midwife in the queue and I whispered in her ear. I said 'Would you like to come into the sluice, and be really dirty and have sex with me? Vulgar sex, like the worst sex you've ever had?'.

She whispered back, 'Doctor Lowry, how dare you, you revolting young man, go away and wash your mouth out with soap and water. And have an enema at the same time.'

I went to the second midwife and whispered the same in her ear, 'Would you like to come into the dirty sluice and have really torrid sex with me, and I'll do this and I'll do that?'

She whispered back, 'Doctor Lowry you naughty man, don't you...' and walked off in a huff.

I went all the way down the line whispering the same sort of thing into each midwife's ear in turn and getting the same kind of firm rejection every time.

I finally got to Sister Beans and I whispered to her, 'Sister Beans, would you like to come to the canteen and let me buy you a cup of coffee?'

She was absolutely ecstatic because nobody had ever done this before to her, she murmured back conspiratorially, 'Oh yes, wonderful.'

As we walked back down the line I sauntered behind her giving all queue of midwives a triumphant thumbs-up sign. Her reputation was gratifyingly ruined and I was the toast of the doctor's residence for weeks after.

Eventually you come to the end of your hospital training and venture into the world outside. I missed the intensity of the labour ward but was beginning to realise I wouldn't relish keeping that pace or work up for the rest of my professional life. But even practicing O&G outside didn't turn out to be any more satisfying as I found out soon after on my first day in the family planning clinic.

It was my first Dutch cap fitting and I was sweating. I had been qualified as a doctor only a month or two and I was acquiring some postgraduate qualifications. Today it was the final practical when I fitted my first barrier contraceptive over the cervix, a rubber Dutch cap smeared with lubricating jelly.

The Dutch cap was a barrier method of contraception. The barrier method relies on preventing the male sperm from ever fertilising the female egg by keeping them physically apart even though Mother Nature was trying her best to unite them.

The method was as described: a barrier of some sort was placed in the way of the sperm which was the element on the move after ejaculation. Barriers could be placed over the penis (the condom) or against the cervix of the female uterus (the sponge, the Dutch cap). The male condom was applied by one or both parties to the sexual act. This had its drawbacks; it might be applied carelessly in the heat of the moment and fail. But the advantage was that the condom didn't need an expert to fit it. This was a major feature of the Dutch cap.

Imagine a dome-shaped rubber cup about the size of a standard drinking cup. That was a Dutch cap. The rubber made it pliable so it would fit snugly against the neck of the female womb, helped by a lavish quantity of lubricant jelly. The woman would normally fit the contraption herself once she had got the hang of it. Some progressive women got their partners to help, but most did it on their own as they wanted to get it in position at the most advantageous time – not too early and not too late. The success of the method did depend a lot on getting the timing right.

The Dutch cap had to be installed first time by an experienced clinician who made sure it fitted, that the woman's anatomy and personal skills were appropriate and that she could manage the technique satisfactorily. So learning to fit a Dutch cap was an important part of a doctor's training if you wanted to provide contraceptive advice.

The theory and the DRCOG examination were behind me. Exams haunt the doctor long after you have qualified and the DRCOG (Diploma of the Royal College of Obstetrics and Gynaecology) was the post-graduate certificate to get to show that you were qualified to provide contraceptive advice and services. In the UK at the time, doctors didn't need to be that well qualified. This was an eye-opener to me and one of the big differences between medicine and dentistry. Doctors seemed to get away with a lot without formal qualifications (I nearly said murder and that was true as well) whereas dentists were kept in check. For example, dentists were beginning to use intravenous sedation for their patients but there was a big fuss made over whether they were safe to do it, what sort of extra training they needed and what supervision they would have to have.

A big song and dance was made over the disputed territory between sedation and general anaesthesia. Dentists were gradually being stripped of their general anaesthesia privileges and being encouraged to use sedation instead. But doctors could till render patients unconscious even if they had never had a day's training in anything to do with safety.

I saw the contrast when I was a GP trainee. We were scheduled to do an anal stretch in the practice, an operation usually done in hospital under general anaesthesia. The procedure involved manually stretching the patient's anal sphincter violently to cure a split in the skin called a fissure. You wanted to be out cold if you were on the receiving end of that.

As I had studied outpatient general anaesthesia extensively as a dentist I said to my doctor trainer that I would check out the equipment, expecting to find emergency oxygen, aspirators, airways and the like. He looked quizzically at me and said there was none of that. He then got the patient in and quickly injected the most potent knock-out drug known to doctors. The victim was completely unconscious and having his anus stretched before I could catch my breath.

He survived but I still don't know how. My trainer broke all the safety rules I had had drummed into me but didn't seem to bother. There was I in dental practice, petrified to give even a homeopathic dose of the weakest sedative surrounded by health and safety belt-and-braces; here was he giving a neat, industrial strength knockout injection with only a fly swat as backup.

I was terrified but it went without a hitch. I swore I would never go that far out on an anaesthetic limb ever again. The patient was alive and pleased: he got his anal stretch and it cured his cough (he daren't cough for weeks). And I learnt what distinguished dentists from doctors: it was assumed that dentists knew nothing but doctors knew everything. Neither rule applied absolutely.

Contraceptive services were one of the exceptions to this. You really had to seek further qualifications so I just had to get the infernal rubber cap to go where it was supposed to go and I could complete my Family Planning Certificate. But the damn thing wasn't co-operating. And my patient didn't help.

Embarrassingly she was vaguely known to me, not the complete stranger I had banked on. So she was trying really hard to co-operate, relax, well, enjoy it. But she had let herself go, so-to-speak, and she had that far-away look in her eyes that rang alarm bells in both me and the sister standing by the instrument tray. And my clumsiness wasn't helping.

The more I fumbled, the more slippery and uncontrollable became the cap. And the patient's writhing wasn't helping now. Then, all of a sudden, it was gone (the cap, not the patient). It shot away like a bar of soap. It sailed over my shoulder and off into oblivion. Trying hard to preserve scrub (and my dignity), I searched frantically all over the floor. They never asked questions on this in the exam.

Up to that point, I thought I would be better at this game than your run-of-the-mill, first-time clinician doctor, what with my dental experience and my advanced years. And, I argued to myself, my dental training would help here in family planning, especially at the practical stuff. For example, I was used to working in an ill-lit cavity, awash with mucous, and some of the materials (rubber, plastic, string) were meat and drink to the dentist.

But this time I was beaten.

I did eventually find the errant Dutch cap later, long after my dignity had shrivelled up entirely. As I said to the sister at the time, 'Well it was your own fault; you shouldn't have had your mouth open'.

18

All this lead me to believe I wouldn't make it in the clinical world of obstetrics, gynaecology or for that matter any mainstream branch of the profession, medical or dental. I was too old to climb the clinical ladder and expect to get to a senior position before I had to retire. I started to look for an alternative career in the health care business that would suit me. I was to end up in public health but on the way I had a look at forensic medicine.

All doctors have to do some forensic medicine. During my senior officer time I arranged to see what went on in the post-mortem room with the local forensic pathologist. I joined a group of trainees as they were shown a typical autopsy. We were taken down into the post-mortem room and the forensic pathologist was going to show us a case.

The room was everything you see on those American television shows about murders and the forensic detective work that goes in to solving all those cases. The room was full of tables, row after row, and the tables each had an old sheet on. He lead us to one specific table and, rather like a matador waving his cape, he pulled back the sheet. All that was on the table was a bootlace with a bit of gristle on it.

We said, 'Well, what on earth is this? Where's the body?'

The pathologist smiled knowingly and said, 'I'll explain. There was a man who was delivering high explosives nearby. He had a van full of dynamite, plastic explosive etc., and he'd gone over a very deep pothole and the track rod end had fallen out of his engine, come through and set off all the explosives. Massive explosion. And this was all they found of him a half-a-mile away. This was the only bit of his body left. And that's his ring piece.'

All that was left of the poor victim was his anal sphincter, his ring piece, and it had what appeared to be his bootlace through it.

We said, 'Well, how do you explain that?'

The Pathologist continued, 'Being a forensic pathologist, you know, you can work things out. What happened was he was obviously driving along with his left foot under his seat. And boom - it's not a very nice way to go with your left boot shoved up your arse at four miles a second.' The satisfied look on his face said it all for me – he was very pleased to have solved the puzzle but had precious little sympathy for the poor victim who had experienced the leather enema. I didn't want to become that callous. And I didn't fancy spending the rest of my career looking at body bits so I sought professional help.

I went to see the dean of the medical and dental faculty at the university.

The dean said, 'What are you going to do?'

I said, 'Look, I could do medicine and dentistry, couldn't I? I could do anything. I could do anything I want.'

He said, 'Have you ever thought about putting people to sleep?'

I said, 'Anaesthetics?'

He said, 'No, public health (it's so boring).' So I went and had a look at public health

What is public health? One widely published definition includes 'the science and art of preventing disease, prolonging life and promoting health through the organised efforts and informed choices of society, organisations, public and private, communities and individuals'. It is involved with threats to the overall health of a community based on analysis of population health whatever the size. It is classically split into epidemiology, biostatistics and health services and may include related fields such as environmental and occupational health. If that's the case then why have public health doctors been tarred with the brush that they are only interested in drains and toilets?

What do you call yours? The thunderbox, the loo, the privy, the netty, the WC? Whatever your pet name for the lavatory, it is still not something to be discussed openly in polite society. So it is left to those whose job it is to look into such matters to take a professional interest in things most people would like to put behind themselves. And if tradition is anything to go by, public health doctors seem to have more than a passing interest in drains and their disgusting contents.

Tradition has it that public health doctors are only interested in things you can catch, and drains. And there was some substance behind that notion, certainly in years gone by. For it was through poor hygiene that many people suffered disease and death until comparatively recently.

So many public health doctors of old spent a lot of their time worrying about human sewerage and what to do with it. Indeed many of the killer diseases we read about in our history books began to retreat not because of advances in medicine but because of improvements in housing, water supply and sewerage disposal. Very different for today's public health people, but they still take a pride in the success of our forefathers. So it was not surprising when I looked at public health that drains and toilets featured that day.

I had wangled an attachment to a public health doctor. He was giving me the hard sell about public health as a career when we were interrupted. A woman came into his office and she put her hat on his desk. She said, 'What are you going to do about that?'

The public health doctor and I then noticed that there was an unmistakable smell of urine from the hat. My colleague spoke: 'That's human urine, isn't it?'

'Yes,' she said, 'I was going down the town past those old fashioned men's toilets when I got showered by human urine as I was walking minding my own business.'

The boss said, 'I know exactly what's happened. The lunchtime drunks were in there and it was highest up the wall for a pound. And one of them has got the airbrick and it's come through and showered your hat.'

So she said, 'Are you going to punish him then?' And the public health doctor sealed the deal for me as the career when he answered, 'No need. If the drink doesn't get him, the diabetes will.' Now that was my kind of specialty. I went and trained in public health and that is what I chose as my definitive career.

Today's public health practitioners worry about more than drains and I spent a long career being a public health doctor and dentist to many populations. I even ended up a university academic. So you could say I have been around a bit and done a lot of things. Some will accuse me of being a Jack-of-all-trades but that was a strength not a weakness. As you will have seen during my training, doctors and dentists used to pride themselves in a well-rounded education. The trend now is for narrowness. I think society will live to regret it if we don't allow some people to have the sort of variety of experience I have had. I don't regret it and I think I made good use of it.

19

People often ask me how come I came to do medicine and dentistry. You now know the real story. It was a search for identity and a purpose in life. It was a cure for desperation. I was desperate to get through my exams and I did eventually. I was desperate to become a professional and I ended up as a member of two. I was desperate to find out my niche in life and I did in the end. I was desperate to grow up and I eventually did. I was desperate for sex and rest assured dear reader that I eventually got what I deserved. But when I am asked what drove me to do dentistry and medicine I play up the 'desperate for sex' angle mainly for laughs.

I say the reason I became a doctor and a dentist was <u>all</u> down to sex. You see, when I was a young man, it wasn't the done thing to go into a pharmacist's and ask for condoms, particularly if there was a young woman serving behind the counter. So picture the scene back then: as I walked into the pharmacist, the young lady says, 'Anything to go, sir?'

I said, 'Yes, I'll have a co-co-co- Colgate toothbrush.'

Six months later I owned enough toothbrushes to turn professional. I did, and I went to study dentistry. Now while I was studying dentistry, of course, the whole scene changed. Now it was compulsory to go into a pharmacist and ask for condoms. So after I'd graduated in dentistry, picture the scene again: me in the pharmacist, again. The young lady behind the counter: 'Anything to go, sir?'

Me: 'Yes, a condom please.'

The pharmacist: 'Any toothbrushes, sir?'

Me: 'No, no. Just a condom.' So six months later I was still a virgin because of the terrible halitosis but with enough condoms to turn professional again. I did, and I studied medicine.

So now, now I've studied medicine and dentistry, I am completely qualified to go into a pharmacist's and ask for what I need. Picture the scene now: 'Do you need anything to go, sir?' –

Me: 'Yes, a ruddy laxative.'

That story about sums it all up. I thought I was going to get my end away but I managed to miss the sexual boat every time during my training. I took a long time finding my ultimate career for all the wrong reasons, but it all turned out right in the end. I have had a cracking good time as both a doctor and a dentist. Although professional life is not primarily for the amusement of the participants, it helps if you enjoy it along the way. And my experiences have given me further pleasure talking about them years later on the conference platform and after dinner. But even that (talking about it rather than doing it) can be fraught with danger.

As a newly qualified dentist, I was invited to speak on false teeth to a pensioner group. I took an example of the latest dental fixative, Dr Wernet's super adhesive, 'guaranteed to keep your upper set firm even in a hurricane'. It was messy stuff and it got all over my inexperienced and sweaty hands. I paid the price when I came to shake hands with the chairman at the end. It took ten minutes to prize us apart. I only wish the dentures I made were as gripping as our two hands. But even the experienced presenter can be caught short.

When I was a junior doctor my boss was the toast of the postgraduate lecture circuit. I used to be his roadie carrying the slide collection, a hip flask and medical specimens. He used to boast that he made his presentations memorable. They were usually unforgettable as he would try to shock his audience for effect.

Out of the blue I got a letter from a hotel where we had appeared months before (his assistants dealt with the admin side, usually arguments over the size of his fee). The hotel manager's letter was curt: 'we know what it is and why you brought it. But where the heck is it?' I knew precisely what he was talking about: it was a pathological specimen he had asked to be passed round the audience, a rotting piece of human flesh beyond description.

I had wondered what had happened to it when we returned to base empty-handed. It turns out a helpful member of the audience had taken it out of the room and hidden it behind the radiator in the dining room. According to the manager, the lunchtime quartet pianist was now regularly passing out from the smell. So no encores for us at that venue. But at least that specimen was harmless enough.

The same hotel was used to the perils of the speaker intent on making an impression. The rather unusual serving hatch in the dining room was the result of a talk by a retired explosives expert who grabbed the live version of a rocket launcher prop by mistake on his way to the engagement. Several elderly members of the audience complained of ringing in the ears for years afterwards and the chef never bent to look in the oven again.

I hope we meet some time socially. You can tell me about your funny stories of dentistry, medicine or your own particular calling. We are all patients/clients/customers in the end so it helps to have a laugh about it all and maybe that eases the pain.

It certainly has for me.

20

Finally, the following document might explain the origins of all the adventures detailed in the pages of this book.

The Apprentice Dentist: Log book of a young English dentist graduating in the 1890s

This is a remarkable manuscript. A recent find, it has been hidden from view (for reasons that will become obvious) since it was written in the late nineteenth/early twentieth century. Judging by the details of life it records at the time, often of a low nature, it was probably never intended for publication. The manuscript, seemingly the only copy ever produced, has lain buried in the archives of the dental school in Newcastle upon Tyne. It was only recovered by chance during a clean-out of some dusty old files at the time of yet another health service reorganisation. Fortunately it was spotted for what it is, a detailed description of the first years in dental practice of one Percival Pitts.

Percival was one of the first students at the newly formed dental school in Newcastle upon Tyne. Dentistry was becoming a newly-regulated profession in an attempt to rid the country of dental quacks and charlatans. As part of that process, newly qualified dentists were asked to record their experiences when they left dental school to start an apprenticeship with an established dentist undertaking a voluntary tutelage. The log of experiences that is recorded by Percival and his contemporaries was used to assure the teachers of the new licentiates that the basic skills taught at dental school were being built upon before they set up as independent practitioners.

Young Pitts went further than was expected. Not only did he record the procedures he carried out in practice; he also recorded his thoughts and feelings and his adventures in and out of his master's dental surgery. And it was some of these adventures, read with increasing alarm by his post-graduate tutor at the dental school that led to all record of his exploits being erased from the existing official dental files, log books and so on and it was only recently that they were revived.

Even Percival's existence was destroyed as part of a nearly-successful attempt to shield the goings-on he recorded in his log. Indeed, if you look at the official records, only one student was said to have been the first to graduate from the school. And if the long-lost log book had been thrown out when it might have been we might never have known of his existence or his exploits.

No-one knows why the log-book was kept at all. Perhaps the dental powers-that-be couldn't believe some of its contents or thought it might be used in evidence to get Percival erased from the dental register should the inevitable falling foul of the law happen. Or perhaps someone in authority was party to the exploits, or found them amusing or titillating enough to preserve them for his own amusement.

So here they are, a unique record of a young man's graduation into the mature dentist he became and the parallel graduation in the university of life in the raw that was Percival's privilege.

7 July 1895
Warm.
Lanchester Guardian offers readers new-fangled package holidays to Whitley Bay.

I am to be apprenticed to a Newcastle dental surgeon, a Mr Ar*****d G**y' of Eldon Square. The Square is situated in the centre of the city, and this prime position gives the practice kudos with potential patients working and living in the nearby shops, offices and more affluent suburbs. (Note added later: This was his main practice. I was to work in a much shabbier branch practice in N*N street).

Today, I attended the surgery for an interview with my prospective employer. The appearance of the premises bodes well for my career: the square is lined with elegant houses of many stories, and Mr G**y's was no exception. As I climbed the stone steps to the heavy front door, I could already see myself receiving patients from the highest strata of society, earning an enviable reputation as a dentist to the gentry and moneyed classes of this fair city.

The practice occupied the ground floor of the house, the front a waiting room, the rear the surgery itself. I was shown into the waiting room by a rather stern lady who I later learnt was the principle's wife. As I settled myself in an expensive leather chair near the coal fire, I noticed the only other occupant of the room, an attractive young woman with a rather forward expression. Though we exchanged little conversation at first, every time I stole a glance at her she would smile and wink at me in a most familiar fashion. At first I thought we must be acquainted but was at a loss to place her pretty face. Then she spoke.

'So the master takes to the boys as well, does he?'

'Pardon?'

'Are you here to be filled or do the filling to put it in dental parlance?'

'Neither' said I, not really understanding the drift of her conversation. 'I'm here to learn the ropes'.

'Oh, my sister and I won't be tied up, however generous the customer is prepared to be. No, there's nothing lewd for us. Everything straight, that's us'.

'Oh, I see', I said, quite relieved when I realised her sister must be having misplaced teeth realigned. And thinking to encourage my companion to help me guess the clinical conundrum being corrected behind the surgery door, I inquired 'Troubled by crowding is she, your sister?'

'Oh strictly one at a time, as I say, we don't indulge in fancy f...' Just then, the door was flung open, and (I presume) the sister entered the room with a somewhat dishevelled appearance. Without pausing to readjust her dress to cover her modesty she entreated her sister to join her in leaving the premises. I had scarcely time to bid them farewell but they kindly offered me their services any time I cared, though to this day I know not what they did for a living.

After waiting for someone to come and escort me into my interview for a full five minutes, I moved to the surgery door which had remained ajar and undisturbed since the sisters had left. I opened the door quietly so as not to startle the occupant and stepped in.

A middle-aged man in a frock coat knelt by the dental chair, and if my eyes did not deceive me, he appeared to be sniffing the seat. However the smile on his face was soon replaced by a scowl when he noticed me. He scrambled to his feet muttering something about losing the lens from a monocle, and then he began to address me as if I were a patient. But as soon as I made it clear I was here in my capacity as a potential apprentice he recovered his composure. He then proceeded to interview me and, though I remember little of the conversation, I must have satisfied him, for he hurried me out of the front door offering me the position if I promised to keep matters to myself in relation to the two girls and especially in front of his wife.

So began my dental apprenticeship.

7 August 1897

Heat wave (well for the North East), icicles glinting in the bright sun.

Assizes busy with sheep rustling cases (Ram-raiders according to the newspapers), apparently big business in these parts.

To the quayside to celebrate my becoming a dentist. Uncle Walter has promised to show me a good time: or as he puts, 'before you put on the professional mantle, you must light the libidinous candle', whatever that might mean.

Uncle Walter is now in his 50s. He lives in London, but says he 'likes to get out of the place, let the soreness diminish, the rash disappear, the itches subside'. I think he has been a debaucher in his youth though he is reluctant to talk of details. Yet I am fond of the old roué, and he me; it was he who encouraged me to record all my experiences in this log book 'warts and all' as he put it.

So it is with some trepidation that I accept his offer to paint the town red (though he says 'gentian violet might be more the colour, if we score'). Alas, a night of shove halfpenny or some other boring tavern game doesn't sound exciting to me and not as I imagine Uncle Walter at all. It might involve shoving, oh yes, but not a halfpenny I'll be bound.

So we set off from his lodging house after darkness had fallen, and presently he ushered me into licensed premises down on the river bank. It was a low dive: any lower and it would have been under water. 'Right' said Uncle Walter, 'here we are bound to get some crumpet'.

'But' said I, 'I want something more substantial than bread'.

'And so you shall' replied he as we were escorted to a table by a charming young woman who seemed to know Uncle Walter from before. But I felt sorry for the poor lass. She struggled in a rabbit-styled costume that was far too tight for her: every time she heaved a sigh of relief, Uncle Walter sighed a heave of relief as he stared at her button-hole area, presumably looking for a name-tag.

As we sipped our first ale, Walter began 'Well my boy, where do you begin this noble art of dentistry? Got a place to hang your plate?' I was about to tell him about the man I was to be apprenticed to when he made an excuse and escorted a young lady up to her chamber. She must have been tired. After a while, when he did not return and with no money to keep my tankard full, I set off in search of him upstairs.

He wasn't in the first room I entered but a young woman was, and she was in bed. Before I could apologise and make my excuses, she spoke. 'So, young master, you've come to see me on a professional basis'. At last, I thought, my first domiciliary consultation: Uncle Walter has told her I am a dentist, and she wishes me to examine her mouth. But when I asked her to open wide, she exposed herself in a most uncomely way. I had to cover my eyes, for it would have been ungentlemanly to look even if I had desired to.

Just then, Uncle Walter entered the room, took me out of the room by my elbow and closed the door saying 'If you have not use for this woman perhaps I can oblige. Your lesson for the night, young Percival: never look a gift whore's mouth, go south'.

10 September 1897
Wet.
William B****s tried for body-snatching but acquitted when discovered he is an undertaker.

The surgery I share with my master is quite unlike those in the Dental School. Where there we worked at chairs set out in long rows in a high-ceilinged room, the surgery at N*n Street more resembled a living room, and one of a wealthy merchant at that.

As you entered the room (the size of a domestic parlour) immediately in front of you, in the middle of the room, was the patient's chair, and though it was upholstered in velvet, that could not disguise the fact that it was made out of heavy cast metal. It looked and was strong and sturdy, ready to resist the rowdiest and protracted wrestling match with a recalcitrant molar in a Keelman's jaw.

By the left arm was a round metal spittoon, with a glass-holder on one side, and a small mushroom-shaped pump handle on the other, which operated a flushing system, although I soon learnt that too enthusiastic use of the mechanism meant I had to empty the chamber too often otherwise it overflowed or smelled or both. Also by the chair was the instrument table on which we laid hand instruments and medicament jars, forceps, mouth gags etc.

A foot drill stood behind the dentist's right shoulder, behind was an open fire, a welcome comforter in the cold, to one side of which was an enamel pedestal wash-hand basin, to the other side a glass-fronted cabinet. In the comer was our gas machine, its cylinders hanging down like pendulous fruit on a tree.

Facing the patients chair was a large cabinet shaped like a roll-topped desk with a marble working surface on which cements were mixed and filling materials dispensed. Remaining space was devoted to a hat-stand and bookshelves containing outdated but impressive-looking tomes. The floor was covered by a Persian rug, something we regretted after a bloody battle with a patient made violent by a stormy general anaesthetic.

Next door to the surgery was where the dental mechanic worked, a purpose-kitted laboratory with work bench, lathe and pressure vessels for vulcanite rubber.

It was back-breaking work bending over the side of the chair to work in the patient's mouth. Although there was a headrest that was adjustable there was little we could do to make the patient's mouth very accessible so lean, stoop and twist it was, patient after patient, week after week. It was not uncommon, on a foggy Friday night in November, for crowds to be seen fleeing a stooped and cursing monster, whereas it was only some weary dentist on his way home in the gloom, hunch-backed by his chair-side work, and maddened and gibbering from an overdose of mercury from the fillings. His only relief might be to allow himself a reviving sniff or two of the nitrous oxide before he set off for his welcoming fireside.

25 November 1887

So cold have asked dental technician to devise an anti-chattering damper for the more expensive dentures.

Thos Ga**age tried for lewd behaviour with a goat. Giving evidence, the arresting constable informed the court unfortunate beast was destroyed 'in case it got a taste for it'.

Quackery still a problem for the unsuspecting public and for us genuine dentists. The Dentists Act (1878) still allows charlatans to practice dentistry provided they don't call themselves dentists. So they fool the public under the guise of 'dental specialists', 'dental consultants', and operate from 'dental parlours', and advertise false teeth in the newspapers. When an unsuspecting member of the public falls into their clutches, an untrained woman in a nurse's uniform lures them into the consulting room, where they are separated from their money by means of trickery: being shown ugly 'cheap' teeth, luxurious expensive alternatives, and by having an upper incisor extracted at the first visit to ensure the unfortunate patient's return.

Mmm, worth a try.

8 December 1897

Shall not bother recording weather unless not cold.

Took morning off and to console myself decided to go to the music hall in N****n^s street. Just before the entrance is a new establishment, 'The Olde Worlde Computer Shoppe', though me thinks is just a new-fangled abacus. The Music Hall was disappointing, featuring one Billy Donnelley, a foul mouthed Scot who plucked the lute and talked of nothing but flatus and fornication.

On way to my lodgings, called at new department store, Fen****s, where a Northumbrian piper now accompanies you around, playing suitable music to get *you in the mood (to spend more money no doubt). Amused when he played 'Greensleeves' in the gardening section, smiled in the bedding department when he performed 'Away in a manger', irritated by 'The nut cracker suit' where they sell trusses and sickened enough to leave the store when, in the menswear department, he played 'Donald where's your trousers' as sung by Mr Donnelley. I predict without fear of contradiction that song will disappear in to the oblivion it deserves.*

The Vulcanite pressure vessel in the laboratory exploded. Glad to report there were no fatalities though good and bad came of the accident in equal measure. It was good that the mighty bang has cured my master's chronic constipation though in too precipitate a fashion necessitating an urgent tailor's appointment.

The worst of it was I nearly lost my fingers, as, when the conflagration erupted, I was trying in Mrs Fort***qe's porcelain teeth. I barely got my fingers out of the way when, with a showering of porcelain splinters, her jaws clamped together in fright, and I'll have to start all over again as soon as her jaws stop quivering.

You will not be surprised to learn that Percival Pitts was a relative of mine.

ABOUT THE AUTHOR

Dr Lowry BDS, MB ChB, DRCOG, FFPH, a qualified doctor and dentist, completed formal training in public health and became an NHS consultant in 1990. Until he retired in 2010 he was a senior lecturer in dental public health at the University of Newcastle upon Tyne and a Fellow of the Faculty of Public Health. He has published over 50 articles in the learned press. He was the training programme director for public health in the Northern Region and an examiner for the Faculty of Public Health. He now devotes most of his working time to teaching, consultancy, humour and after-dinner speaking. This may seem an odd mixture but he has penned comedy for radio, television and the press and he has a regular column in a newspaper. His first book was 'Be an entertaining speaker'.

www.drlowryafterdinnerspeaker.co.uk

Printed in Great Britain
by Amazon